Tena Huizenga

Tena Huizenga
Missionary to Nigeria, 1937-54

Shawn Brix

Van Raalte Press

A. C. Van Raalte Institute, Hope College

Van Raalte Press is a division of Hope College Publishing

A. C. Van Raalte Institute
Theil-Nyenhuis Research Center
9 East 10th Street
PO Box 9000
Holland, MI 49422-9000

https://hope.edu/vri
vanraalte@hope.edu

Printed in the United States of America
Library of Congress Control Number: 2023946590

Editor-in-Chief and Publisher
        Jacob E. Nyenhuis, PhD

Project Editor
        JoHannah M. Smith

Digitization, editing, and layout
        Paul A. Heusinkveld

This book was originally published in 1994 with the title "In the Master's Service," by Calvin Theological Seminary, Grand Rapids, Michigan. The Van Raalte Institute is indebted to Calvin Theological Seminary and Shawn Brix for being able to republish the book and make it available in this new updated edition.

Van Raalte Press

In memory of Peter H. Huizenga, whose vision was to document Dutch heritage and God's work among Dutch immigrants in North America.

The Missionary Memoirs Series of the Van Raalte Press, no. 6

This series is dedicated to publishing the heretofore untold stories of missionaries of the Reformed Church in America and the Christian Reformed Church in North America and Hope College alumni who worked to proclaim the Christian Gospel, both at home and abroad. These books are the recorded accounts of their experiences, transformational for themselves and the people of the countries where they served.

Series Editor
>Donald A. Luidens, PhD
>Director, Van Raalte Institute

Project Editor
>JoHannah M. Smith
>Van Raalte Institute

Editor-in-Chief and Publisher
>Jacob E. Nyenhuis, PhD
>Director Emeritus, Van Raalte Institute

Editorial Board
>The Albertus C. Van Raalte Research Professor and
>the Senior Research Fellows of the Van Raalte
>Institute

Contents

Illustrations

Acknowledgments

This project represents an ideal form of cooperation—a tripartite relationship between the private sector, the seminary, and the church. It is a wonderful example of what we in seminary administration call "the scholarship of service." This book has appeared because patrons of faith and vision who are concerned that a sense of Christian service be inspired in the next generation made the resources available to complete it. It was suggested and superintended by us at Calvin Theological Seminary, which provided the academic guidance as well as the research and writing expertise needed to do it well. It exists for individual Christians, congregations, mission agency personnel, archivists, leaders of the Nigerian church, and all others eager to learn of the church's attainments in the name of Christ.

I thank Mr. Peter Huizenga of Oakbrook, Illinois, and the trustees of the Elizabeth I. Huizenga Foundation for their encouragement, counsel, and generosity. This is the second such project that they have sponsored through us.

I thank Mr. Herman Kanis for working with me on behalf of the Huizenga family to set the wheels in motion and to assist so ably with overseeing every stage of the project.

I thank Mr. Shawn Brix, the seminary graduate who undertook the research so diligently and did such a creative job in conceiving and writing the book. It was a joy to make this opportunity available to him and to see him further develop his obvious skills through it.

I thank the people whom Mr. Brix interviewed extensively in gathering data and answering pertinent questions; their record is invaluable, and their testimonies are preserved to some degree through this study.

I thank the printers for their advice and cooperation on design and publication.

And above all I thank God, whose Spirit moving in the soul and life of Tena Huizenga, made this story of dedication and achievement possible and worth telling to those who will benefit significantly from it.

Dr. James A. De Jong
President, Calvin Theological Seminary
(1994)

Preface

"Who will go for me?" "Here am I, send me." These words were exchanged between the Almighty and the prophet Isaiah. The results of Isaiah's "Send me" continue to affect the world even today. Many people have felt a strong desire inside to answer 'a call' and do something in response to the needs of people: people who are suffering because of their separation from God. For some this desire is never satisfied because it is snuffed out by the little whispers, "You can't make a difference," or, "The cost is too great." This true story about Aunt Tena clearly reenforces the truth that one person, obedient to and trusting in God, can make a difference. My prayer is that some who read it will say, "I have that desire. Here am I, send me."

Aunt Tena's story is even more meaningful when we consider the time in which her life began. Women in the Dutch community during the early decades of this century did not have the freedom of choice and opportunity that is available today. Aunt Tena, as did those who preceded her to Nigeria, "broke the mold" when she accepted God's call to do something beyond the ordinary and expected. There was a price to pay as a result of her decision. The price was leaving family, church, and the comfort of friends and familiar surroundings, to take a life journey into a world about which she knew very little and to a people who were as different from her as daylight is from dark. All this became more and more weighty as the time drew near for her departure. But God, who called her, gave her grace for the task. Part of this grace came in the form of loving support and encouragement from the people already in the field and from the family she left behind. This will be evident throughout this story of an ordinary person who did extraordinary things as God led and enabled her. You are about to embark on an adventure as you read. Live the story in your imagination; it will deepen your appreciation of Tena's life and, in a sense, you will meet a Tena you didn't know.

In addition to this being Tena's story, this period was a high point in the history of the Christian Reformed Church, as all across this denomination there was vision, vitality, and commitment to the historic Reformed faith in the ordinary believer. This spiritual incubator "hatched" young people with a desire to answer God's call to full time service. This also enabled a work such as this to be launched and carried on. The average church member had a faith that was practical and needed to be lived out every day. Part of this practice was the support of missions. As we learned from the book *Daughters Who Dared* by Gerald Zandstra (page 47), it was this grass roots support, spiritual zeal, and dedication that was the undergirding which enabled these women, without CRC denominational endorsement or support for the first 20 years, to continue and expand their work. This is another illustration of the truth that when God calls, He also provides.

Herman Kanis
(1994)

Introduction

I had been working on this project for several months when I found myself at my desk one night with my eyes full of tears. I had already read and reread several years worth of entries from Tena's diaries and travel logs describing her joys and struggles during her missionary years. I had also worked my way through over 20 years of letters between Tena and her brother Pete, who faithfully corresponded with her all the time she was in Nigeria. But it was a letter that Tena wrote to Pete in 1953, expressing her love and appreciation for all he had done for her, that finally caught me with a lump in my throat. It was at that moment that I knew I had entered Tena's life in some small way.

As a result, although I was never able to meet her, I feel that Tena has made an impact in my life. She has challenged me once again to commit myself wholeheartedly to the Master's service, and has reminded me of the importance of family and friends along life's journey.

In Tena's story, I hope that you too will find an ordinary yet remarkable woman.

Shawn Brix
(1994)

CHAPTER 1

A Labor of Love Bears Fruit

In 1969, Tena Huizenga had already been back in the United States for a decade and a half after serving for seventeen years as a medical missionary in the Benue Province of Nigeria. After an initial adjustment period that had been difficult, she had settled back into the American way of life. She had not, however, forgotten the Nigerian church and its people. She continued to pray for the work she had helped begin there, and for the people she had come to know and love. She kept in contact with the Christian Reformed Church's Foreign Mission Board with regards to policy changes, as well as challenges and successes on the missionary field. She also continued to give generously to the work of the Nigerian Church. She sent money to the Takum and Mkar hospitals, to the Nigerian Theological College, to the Johanna Veenstra Junior Seminary, and to various other causes such as the building of new drinking and irrigation wells.

Neither had the people of Nigeria forgotten her. In April, she received a letter from Yakabu Bete RN, who had just been promoted to the rank of Assistant Nursing Superintendent at the Takum Christian Hospital. He wrote:

> I have to thank you for your remembrance of me, especially in your prayers. Your letter ... reminds me of the love, kindness, patience, and your helping hand you had while you were here with us. I also will never forget that. I always muse upon the good time I had with you

when I was serving as a house boy and a sweeper in the dispensary. I was unable to read and write while I was serving you as a house boy but you allowed me to attend the evening school. Few years after you think I will be better in the ministry of mercy than to serving you alone as a house boy. You put me in the dispensary. There I made many, many mistakes, enough to send me away but you had patience with me ... and kept me with you. The work in the dispensary was growing and they were looking for a boy to send to Vom. You brought my name to the Authority. I was sent to Vom in 1942 for this urgency need. I came back home in six weeks: time to help you with leprosy work. I was sent to Vom again in 1945, during the second World War, to learn how to diagnose and treat the other common tropical diseases. I stayed there three years and six months. I came back to Lupwe in June 1948. I work with you ...

To you all I indeed owe a deep debt of gratitude. I know quite well that I did not deserve all that patience, mercy, and love that you have shown me. You did this in order to extend the kingdom of our Lord in Africa, in Nigeria, and in Takum District. Thanks much.

I think it'll be good if you visit us here again and see the fruit of your work. I am sure you will be very impressive by seeing many changes in our area.

Attached to Yakabu Bete's 16-page letter were a number of shorter letters with greetings from his children, nephews, and nieces. One wrote:

Madam,

Many greetings to you in the name of our Lord Jesus Christ. I was just a small boy when you left Nigeria. My father said I was attacked by a bad diarrhea and was almost dead but you helped and prayed much for my survival.

Many thanks!

Another had scrawled from the Government Girl's College in Kano:

Dear Madam,

Much have been hearing about you from our uncle, Yakabu Bete. We thank God that, through you and he, many of us in the family have the privilege of attending high institutions. One of my senior brothers is now studying in over-seas.

Many thanks to you. Greetings to all.

Tena's relationship with the Nigerian Church and people continued throughout the remainder of her life. In 1976, Stephen Ali Bulus wrote affectionately to Tena, calling her his "mother,"

I am very happy to write you these few lines. It is more than ten years I didn't hear of you and you didn't hear of me.

As my mother, I was ashamed to write you, because I sinned against my God ... [But] I am now back to my God and the church have receive me. I am now a full member of the church again.

In my school where I am teaching I am the religious instructor. I have about 246 children who are hearing Word of God everyday. About 60 have been baptized. I am now happy as God has called me back to him.

Please Mother don't forget me in your prayers, so that God may be with me and use me as a tool to bring His people ...

I am sure this letter will be as dream to you, but it is real, I am your lost and found son ... Hoping to hear from you soon as possible, Mother. Your kindness towards me during my school years will not be forgotten Mother. Thank you very much. Thank you, and thank you again.

By the time of her death in 1978, Tena's life had touched not only Yakabu Bete's and Stephen Ali Bulus' life, and the lives of their families but also the lives of many other Nigerians as well.

Similarly, at home her life had also directly impacted the lives of those in her extended family. She brought to her kin a simple lifestyle that emphasized the importance of faith and family ties. She encouraged an attitude of generosity and instilled in all a pride in the family's heritage.

Celebrating Tena's life, an article in the June 16, 1978 issue of the *Banner,* the Christian Reformed Church's denominational publication, asked, 'Truly, who can measure the influence of her life?"

CHAPTER 2

The Early Years

When Harm and Altje Huizenga had their third child on February 26, 1907, it was their first girl. They named her Trientje, but her brothers Siert and Tammes, and everyone else, soon got in the habit of calling her "Tena." The latter name stuck, and Tena was to use it not only as a nickname but also as her name on all official documents and health records as well. She was baptized in March of the same year in the First Christian Reformed Church (CRC) of Chicago, by Rev. E. Breen.

Tena's father, Harm, had struck out to America from his hometown of 't Zandt in the province of Groningen, Holland, when he was 23. Within a year, he had started his own business, hauling waste for $1.25 a load. He had returned to Groningen briefly in 1897 to become married to Altje Kramer on March 17 and, together, they returned to the west side of Chicago to begin the American chapter of the Huizenga clan. Tena's oldest brother, Siert (Sam), was born in January 1898 and, in due time, was followed by a second son for Harm and Altje, Tammes (Tom), born in December of 1901.

Tena's birth in 1907 demanded that the family of five move from their home at 1454 West 14th Street to 1348 South Ashland Avenue. At first they lived together on the first floor, but later the happy clan moved to the second floor. In October of 1908, Harm and Altje were blessed with their fourth child, a boy they named Petro (Peter).

While Harm's family was expanding, his business was following suit and he was able to add more men, wagons, and horses to his waste hauling venture. The family was becoming a respected part of the community, and they were able to enjoy some of the luxuries of life in their new Ashland Avenue home.

Harm's hometown of 't Zandt

Their happy life of family, church, and work, however, was soon to be painfully disrupted. Tena was later to write:

On [Saturday] March 15, 1913, a large funeral procession passed our home, and mother, without a wrap, watched it from the porch. Having worked all morning, she was perspiring freely and caught a cold from this exposure, causing her to be sick the following morning. On Monday the physician was called and he diagnosed the case as Pneumonia. On Tuesday she became unconscious, and on Saturday evening [March 22] at 9:00 P.M., mother was called to be with the Lord.

The following morning Peter and I ran to sit on father's knee, and it was there that he told us that mother had gone to be with Jesus. Just what this meant we did not know, but from the tone of father's voice, we knew it was something of great importance. He then showed us mother, who was laying on the stretcher in the parlor. Pete was only four years, and I was but six years. The funeral of mother was per carriages, and it lasted many an hour.

After mother's death father had a housekeeper to do the work, and her name was Johanna Schoolveld. And it was during this period that we felt the emptiness of our home very much.

Life must not have been easy for Harm, nor for the children. His growing business demanded time to manage, yet he had four children under the age of 15 who missed the love and care of their mother. Harm decided upon a new course of action. Writing to his brother Willem in Holland, he asked, "Do you know of a woman who would make a good wife for me?" Willem assured Harm that a woman in his old hometown of 't Zandt would make him an ideal wife. Aaltje Keizer, a 42 year old baker's daughter who taught students how to knit and sew, had been engaged but her fiancé had died. Hopeful, Harm wrote her, asking her what she thought of marriage and moving to America. Her reply was direct: "I don't know who you are and I have no intention of moving to America." Harm was not put off, however, and late in 1914, with WWI having just broken out, Harm sold his garbage business and household belongings to move his family of four children back to Holland. They arrived in December to the unhappy news that Harm's mother had died only two weeks previous, and that Harm's

Tena and Peter with
their mother Altje

brother Lambert was very sick with dropsy. Mixed in with this despairing news was also a sign of hope: when the family arrived by train to Groningen, Ms. Aaltje Keizer was waiting with Willem to greet them.

Two months later, on February 14, 1915, Aaltje and Harm stood side by side again, this time at the city hall making marriage vows to one another. After the ceremony, the family was ushered into the home of grandfather Bolt where the reception was to take place. Tena never forgot the full-dressed suits and other finery that the relatives wore to that grand celebration.

As was Dutch custom, the marriage ceremony was continued the next day in the church and Tena, along with her brothers, was granted the great honor of being allowed to sit in the minister's pew for the entire service.

Harm and Aaltje bought a home in Bedum, but due to a temporary lack of homes, they were forced to live in the front section. This demanded that Tena and Peter had to stay behind in 't Zandt for a few months but they too were soon able to join the rest of the family.

Tena's years in Holland were among her very happiest. Reflecting on these years, she later wrote,

> In Spring we too went to Bedum, where we had a beautiful home, with everything a child could desire. The home was situated on the banks of a beautiful river, which was a short distance from the village. Consequently we could see all the steamers pass through the river, and in the veranda we had a splendid view over the garden, which terminated into a park.

> The front section of the garden was arranged for flowers and shrubberies, while in the rear we could raise our own vegetables, as well as our own fruit trees.

> Besides this we had a few gymnastic apparatuses, on which we could amuse ourselves. And as we had much company, the older people could use the swing, and the things that went with it. Looking back over these days,

we truly can say that they were the happiest of our childhood, for it was here that we enjoyed life as it can only be enjoyed in a small village, without the care and the hurry and bustle that is so common to a large city.

Tena enjoyed life in Bedum.

Being in the land of her parents' birth also allowed Tena to get to know her extended family. She kept a "Poesie" book so that when relatives or friends visited the house, they could write notes of love and encouragement to her. In 1915, when she was 8 years old, her grandparents wrote to her:

Dear granddaughter

In God's hands you are safe.
He watches over you.
All his ways are wise and holy
He protects you day and night.
He shall lead you in such a way
that you some day have to say,
at the end of my struggle
Lord your way with me was good.
That is the wish from your loving grandparents,
    G. Bolt
    F. Schuit

This prayer and blessing of Tena's paternal grandparents was to be realized throughout her life in sometimes striking fashion.

Tena's last sibling, Gerritt Harry, was born to Harm and his new wife on June 28, 1916. With the German artillery shells of WWI approaching ever closer, the family, now numbering seven, returned to America in October of the same year. Tena's idyllic life in Holland numbered a mere 22 months, while she grew through the tender ages of 8 and 9. Nevertheless, even in this brief span of time, Tena developed a love for the country and its people that she would carry with her throughout her entire life.

Much later, when she was serving in Nigeria, she would sometimes visit Holland on her way back to America for furloughs. She welcomed the opportunity to be able to speak with others in Dutch again, and would hop from home to home in Groningen and elsewhere, gathering the family news. When she arrived in Chicago, she would be eager to share the greetings, information, and gossip from the Huizenga clan on the other side of the Atlantic.

Tena's proficiency in the Dutch language was an ever present source of pride for her, and she lamented the fact that the second or third generation American Huizengas never kept up their "mother tongue." She was always quoting Dutch phrases, songs, and poems to the family, hoping to whet their appetite for the language of their forefathers. She even promised a free trip to Holland for anyone in the family who would take the time to learn Dutch! Despite her jovial teasing and good-hearted encouragement, no one ever took her up on her lucrative offer. Nevertheless, some of the family did make small strides in mastering the foreign tongue. In 1956, Tena's niece Sue wrote her a short note from Calvin College updating her Aunt on her return trip to the campus and thanking her for the books she had sent. The letter was written in Dutch, but had to be prefaced in English with the warning, "First of all, I must tell you that I know my word orders are all wrong, and some of my tenses!" She added, "If you have time, maybe you could send it back in a corrected form, so I would know what I did wrong."

If Tena's love of Holland and its native tongue never resulted in an American Huizenga learning to write or speak fluent Dutch, it did result in an increased appreciation and understanding of the family's history by all. The sense of heritage that she helped instill in the family was largely responsible for the Huizenga reunion that brought together both the American and European halves of the family on Melkema Farm in the town of Huizinge, Holland, in the summer of 1993. Had Tena been alive, she would have been enthralled by the gathering of 250 relatives who together celebrated their past and future as a family on August 6 with a day full of festivities.

Tena

In 1916, when the family returned to America after an 18-day voyage, they traveled to Chicago with the intention of moving back into their Ashland Avenue home. The people who were renting there, however, could not find another place to live. Since Harm still owned both homes, the family moved into their flat on 14th Street—the one with no plumbing! It was not until the following spring that they were able to go to their six room house on Ashland Avenue.

In Chicago, the family quickly settled back into life in America. They again became deeply embedded in the life and work of First CRC, and Tena returned to Ebenezer Christian Grade School. Meanwhile WWI raged on. When the armistice was finally signed in 1918, it cleared the way for Aaltje to return to the Netherlands for an extended visit to her family. Tena was left as "mother" of the house and, as such, developed a special love for "baby Harry" that she never lost.

In the years that followed, Tena worked her way through high school in the evenings at Medill High School and Balfour Johnstone School. It was during these high school years that Tena began to sense that the Lord she loved and served was at work in her life, directing her towards a life that would find her serving others in the name of Jesus Christ.

Tena and her four brothers with father and
grandmother

CHAPTER 3

A Call Comes into Focus

Reverend John Van Lonkhuyzen served the Huizenga's First CRC congregation in Chicago for 10 years from 1918 to 1928. A colorful and forward-looking pastor, Van Lonkhuyzen was clearly Kuyperian in his theology and outlook, and was constantly exhorting his congregation to become integrated into every sphere of society in order to win it for Christ and his kingdom. Through Tena's influential teen years, she sat through his preaching twice each Sunday, hearing his challenge to boys and girls alike to become active outside the home for the sake of Christ.

Tena in her teen years

Tena knew that her parents' expectation was for her to get married, settle down on the west side of Chicago, have a family of her own, and enjoy her family, friends, and community in a more comfortable style than her parents. Yet Van Lonkhuyzen's messages had struck a chord with her, and she decided to test the waters. In 1925, she entered the Chicago Mission Training School for a three year program that required extensive hands-on work. She soon found herself working with the downtrodden of Chicago at the Helping

Hand Mission on Madison Street, a ministry of the Chicago area Christian Reformed churches. It was there that she met the Superintendent of the Mission, John VandeWater. VandeWater's book, *The Street of Forgotten Men: Ten Years of Missionary Experience in Chicago*, reveals the vigor with which he approached his work. As Tena worked alongside him, she began to share his infectious love for the lost.

She also became very involved at the Nathaniel Mission, a Jewish mission on what was then Crawford Avenue in Chicago. Tena was influenced there by the likes of Mr. A. Huisjen, Dr. Jonker, and Mrs. Edith VanderMeulen. Edith, who was seven years older than Tena, was good friends with the Huizenga family and was also a member of the First CRC. There, like Van Lonkhuyzen, she made repeated appeals to the young people to dedicate their lives to the Lord's service.

Johanna Veenstra (*center front*) pioneered the work in Lupwe. She was later joined by Nelle Breen, Jennie Stielstra, and Bertha Zagers (*left to right*).

By the time Tena received her diploma from the Chicago Mission Training School, she knew the Lord was calling her to mission work. Trusting that the Lord wanted her to serve as a nurse, she began her medical training at Garfield Park Hospital as a private duty nurse.

As she practiced her nursing skills, her adventurous spirit and desire to travel had her dreaming of far-off places where she might be able to take her love of Christ and her growing knowledge of healing and medical care. It was during these years of dreaming and praying that Dr. Henry Beets, missions work promoter extraordinaire, kept Tena and the entire CRC abreast of the work that a young woman named Johanna Veenstra was pioneering in the heart of the Benue province in Nigeria. As editor of both the *Banner* and *Missionary Monthly*, Beets wrote of the progress and challenges that faced Miss Veenstra in her work in his editorials and articles. He also regularly published letters and articles by Miss Veenstra herself, and he repeatedly challenged the CRC to take up the cause of her work there.

Tena read these articles with wonder and excitement and when Johanna Veenstra was home on furlough, Tena listened with rapt attention to her speak at churches and Women's Missionary Union meetings in Illinois. Johanna, a CRC member from Paterson, New Jersey, had been in Nigeria since 1920, working under the Sudan United Mission (SUM) at a small mission outpost south of the Benue River at Lupwe. Africa was still known in mission circles then as the "missionary graveyard of the world" and, indeed, when Johanna first set foot in Nigeria, she learned that a missionary had died from malaria only a few days earlier, and that a second woman, a Canadian missionary, had been killed just the previous day by a poisonous snake bite.

Johanna's work in Lupwe was primarily among the Kuteb tribe. Prior to her arrival, these people had borne the name "Dzompere," meaning "Man Eaters" or the name "Muncie," which means "We Eat" in their tribal tongue. The tribe was considered so dangerous that for years the government would not allow missionaries to enter the Kuteb area.

Johanna worked with a British missionary, Miss Clara Haigh, for several years together at Lupwe. Together, they served the peoples surrounding Lupwe in sundry villages as evangelists, teachers, doctors, builders, and agriculturalists. Their pleas for more laborers in the kingdom harvest went unanswered for many years.

In Chicago, Tena's ears perked and her heart stirred as she listened to Johanna tell of the primitive and exhausting medical work on the compound. Skin ulcers and other tropical diseases, eye infections, leprosy, and sleeping sickness were all common ailments among the Kuteb. Furthermore, with an infant mortality rate of more than 50%, prenatal and natal care was greatly needed. She continued to listen as the front-line missionary explained how the medical and educational work efforts at Lupwe helped to promote the evangelism work. The Nigerians were attentive to the message that the "Baturiya" ("white woman") brought and they were beginning to attend the worship services that she and some of the local men led. While the growth of the church was slow, Johanna described how first individuals and then entire families were turning away from their fetish worship, burning both the fetishes and the little houses that they had built for them. At the heart of fetish worship was the conviction that there was a relationship between ordinary objects such as sticks and stones, trees and plants, and the mysterious power of unseen spirits. If a pagan became interested in Mohammedanism, he did not have to break from fetishism entirely, for a bit of Koran wrapped up in a cloth may simply become his new fetish. The good news that Johanna brought freed people from such superstition to serve the Living God. Nevertheless, even for those who believed her message, liberation from superstition was slow. For one who had avoided all his life putting his foot on a certain spot, or touching the branch of a certain tree, it was not easy to completely forget the old taboos.

At the end of the presentation, as Johanna related the need for more workers in order for God's kingdom in Nigeria to continue advancing, Tena wondered if this might be the Lord's call upon her own life.

At the completion of her nurse's training at Garfield Park, Tena entered Moody Bible Institute in Chicago and it was there that she became wholly convinced that it was to Africa that the Lord was calling her. She cherished her studies at the downtown college and, years later, she would still reminisce about the Moody days with other missionaries who had enjoyed the same training. She kept up contact with the school even after she had been in Nigeria many years. She kept a scrapbook in which she placed articles and pictures that portrayed some of the school's ongoing history and important milestones. Some of the letters that she sent to the school to keep them abreast of her work were even read over the Moody airwaves. One of the highlights of her first furlough was traveling home to America from Holland aboard the same ship on which Dr. Ironside from Moody Church was also a

Tribal fetish built in hopes of offering protection.

passenger. He was returning from a convention in Keswick, England, and Tena was thrilled to make his acquaintance. He gave her a small pocket Bible as a souvenir of the trip.

At Moody, she was an ambitious student and she soon became accustomed to the disciplined style of early morning devotions that she was taught there. These devotions would remain an important part of her life, even well beyond her studies. Despite the rigors of student life, however, she still had time for family and good-natured laughter. One weekend, Tena invited her niece Ella to come visit her on campus for a few days. They had fun together, riding on the old wire cage elevators that used to run up and down the shafts in Moody's student housing. The traffic and noise on LaSalle Avenue was so loud that Ella did not sleep either of the two nights she was there!

It was while Tena was at Moody in 1933, that news of Johanna Veenstra's untimely death (just before her 39th birthday) was announced to the CRC through the *Banner*. She was buried in a cemetery near the hospital in Vom, Nigeria, where she had died. Little did Tena know that only five years later she would find herself praying beside Johanna's grave, rededicating her life to the Lord's service and to the work in Lupwe to which she was called.

Sitting there, in what Tena called a "hallowed spot," beside the stone cross that marked where Johanna lay, Tena prayed "May we, who follow in these steps, be faithful to our Sender."

Just five months before Johanna died, she had been joined in the work at Lupwe by three other women from the CRC, all similarly working under the SUM. Bertha Zagers of Fremont, Michigan, was a trained nurse, and Jennie Stielstra of Holland, Michigan, was a trained teacher. Nelle Breen (soon to marry and become Nelle Smith), another teacher from Holland, Michigan, had served with Johanna for two years but was home on furlough when the news arrived that her colleague's heart had failed only days after an appendicitis operation.

Tena graduated from the Moody Bible Institute in 1935.

When Jennie Stielstra returned to America late in 1934 for her first furlough, Tena was only a couple months away from receiving her diploma from Moody and eager to explore the possibilities of joining the team at Lupwe. In a letter dated January 10, 1935, she welcomed Jennie back to the United States, indicating that she had read of her homecoming in the *Banner*. She then invited her to the Windy City for the Founder's Week Conference at Moody, promising her that the speakers would be a blessing to all who attended. As Tena was to express later in the letter, however, there was also an ulterior motive for her invitation:

And then there is also a personal interest in your coming here to the Institute. I have written to Mrs. [Nelle] Smith at different times about the work out in Africa. I feel definitely called to go out to that country, but as yet I have not felt definitely led as to which Mission Board I should go under. I have written to the Sudan Interior Mission and have corresponded with them, but before I connect myself with them I would also like to know whether there might be a possibility of working under the Sudan United Mission. I am going to write to them this evening, and inquire about the possibility of working under their Board. And then there are so many questions that I would like to ask you that it seems unless we could interview one another we might not get through with all that lies on my heart.

Do pray for me especially in this matter. Miss Stielstra, for I do want to be in the center of the Lord's will. I hope to graduate from the Missionary course in August, and I would like nothing better than to be sent out immediately, the Lord willing.

Although Tena was a friend of a teacher with whom Jennie had taught before leaving the States, this was the first contact she had ever made with Jennie personally. It was the beginning of what was soon to blossom into a lifelong friendship.

In February of 1935, Jennie arrived in Chicago and she and Tena were able to have their "heart to heart talk." Only weeks later, Tena would learn that her application to the Sudan United Mission had been approved by their Council. On April 3, she wrote again to Jennie:

By this time you have already heard the decision of the Council in regards to my application. Mingled feelings accompanied the opening of the letter, received from Mr. MacClelland. It seemed too good to be true. At last my hope of becoming an ambassador for Christ was beginning to come true. I truly feel unworthy of this high calling, but feel confident that with Christ I can go forward, knowing that He goeth before me. And although I am just an ordinary person, we have an extraordinary God who will supply all our needs ...

My prayer is that He will use me as a clean empty vessel, to convey His Word to those in darkness. May I be steadfast in this one calling.

Later in the same letter, Tena confided.

At times Satan does tempt me with doubts and fears, and I am not always equally ready to say, "Here am I Lord, send me." But with God's grace I hope to go forward, relying on His promises. I do need your prayers very much, and I can assure you that you too will always be remembered in mine.

Perhaps God's answer to these prayers was to give Tena more time to become assured of her calling and confident of His hand at work in even the smallest details of her life. In July, she found out that, due to a lack of funds, the SUM would not be able to send her out immediately. It would be another year and a half and more before Tena's dream would become a reality and she would set forth for Africa.

CHAPTER 4

Setting Sail

The letter was addressed to Miss Tena Huizenga, dated October 8, 1936, and signed from George R. MacClelland of the American branch of the SUM. The departure of Bertha Zagers from the mission compound at Lupwe left a hole that Tena was to fill. She was to leave for Nigeria in about three months.

Tena just prior to leaving for Nigeria.

Waiting patiently for over a year for this letter to finally arrive, Tena had been taking courses in both midwifery and anesthetics, and clinging to Philippians 3:10, a verse that had become important to her: "I want to know Christ and the power of his resurrection and the fellowship of sharing in his sufferings, becoming like him in death." She had also been recounting Psalm 32:8 to herself: "I will instruct you and teach you in the way you should go; I will counsel you and watch over you."

Also in this time of expectant waiting, she had received a $1,000 pledge for her work from Mr. Savage in Philadelphia, a man that she didn't know and had never met. Half of the money had already been sent and the other half was to be sent when she would sail. This was such a tremendous act of zeal that Tena had seen it as a seal of her appointment to the work from the Lord himself.

Now, however, the waiting and anticipating were over. The preparations for leaving had to begin.

The final weeks were a flurry, with Tena often wondering how she could ever get ready on time. She attended the Founder's Week Conference again at Moody, as she had for the previous two years, and found herself inspired. When Mr. MacClelland wrote on February 9 to inform her that her boat would leave in 18 days, she was unable to sleep that night. She was concerned with having to leave her family behind but she brought her concerns to the Lord in prayer, finally trusting that everything would turn out well.

The next several days were spent packing and shopping for necessities. She gathered some of the outfits and articles that she would be bringing and laid them out on her bed upstairs so that friends and relatives who came by to wish her well would be able to see some of the things that would travel with her to Nigeria.

On February 14, she received a special delivery letter confirming her reservation on the SS *Scythia*, sailing from New York on February 27, 1937 at 11:30 A.M. In her diary that day, Tena wrote,

> A medley of emotions swelled up within me upon this definite news ... I sure had a crying spell this P.M. Was I willing to give up my all at the Master's service? It was true I had longed for it all my life, but now that it was so close I counted the cost. But praise be to the Lord, by His grace I could look up and say, "Here am I Lord, send me."

While she received many gifts and encouraging letters from her family in those final days, she also had some friends try to discourage her from going. Nevertheless, Tena remained resolute in her decision, believing that it was the Lord himself who was calling her.

The evening of February 19 brought a festive party at which the family offered their blessings and well-wishes to the only daughter of the Huizenga family. They gave her a movie camera and several additional gifts: one for almost everyday of the trip that would take her first to Liverpool, England, and then on to Nigeria. Tena's diary indicates that the fellowship of that evening brought to her mind other occasions when the chair that was empty that night had been graced by her "Daddy." Harm had died just 13 months previous from a cerebral hemorrhage at the age of 67. In an article that appeared in the May 1937 issue of *Missionary Monthly*, Tena wrote,

> It was my own mother's prayer that one of her children might go out as a missionary. She did not live to see it, nor did my father who died last year very suddenly, but I owe them much for their prayers and their Christian life, for they influenced me much.

Two days after Tena's farewell party was Sunday and, as always, she celebrated the day in church. In the morning she spoke of her impending work to the children in the Sunday School of First Church and, in the evening, she spoke at another Chicago CRC about the needs of Africa. The church was filled to capacity and a collection was taken for the work. Tena wrote in her diary, "I could tell I was leaving many friends behind." She was grateful, however, for the prayers and support that these friends promised.

Tena and stepmother Aaltje, several years after Tena had left for Africa.

The final few days in Chicago were the toughest. Tena's mother found it difficult to speak of her leaving. Tena too found it impossible to put into words how hard it was for her to go. With her father gone, and her brothers all married, Tena couldn't stop thinking of her mother being left all alone in the family's big house. "But," she wrote in her diary, "somehow or other I feel that God will care for her in a most unexpected way." When her parting with "Ma" finally came on February 24, Tena needed the Lord's strength for she almost wanted to turn back. In her diary, Tena wrote, "Ma took it very hard. God watch over us while we are absent one from another."

Along with her mother, more than 75 others were at the train station to see Tena off. As the train prepared to depart, they sang "God Will Take Care Of You," and 'Take The Name Of Jesus With You," among other hymns of encouragement. As Harry whispered a final farewell in her ear, she boarded the train with her brother Tom and waved goodbye.

The next day they arrived in New York and were met by Rev. Beebe who entertained them at his house that evening and provided their lodging. The next morning, February 26, Tena awoke to her 30th birthday. "Will I ever forget [this] birthday?" she asked in her diary. "I guess not! It was one of my happiest birthdays, even though far from home on my way for services in the darkest continent."

The following day's entry begins, "At last the day has come that I must say farewell to my native land." Rev. Hoogstra took Tom and Tena to the steamer and there they were met by several others, including Rev. Beebe. In a small corner of the dining room on board, the party totaling nine gathered for a short farewell service. Accompanied by Mrs. Dyer on the violin, they again sang "Take The Name Of Jesus With You," and together sought the Lord's blessing in prayer. After some parting remarks and another prayer, the small entourage, including Tom, said their final goodbyes and left the ship. Shortly thereafter, at 11:30 in the morning, the siren of the SS *Scythia* groaned the moment of parting. Moments later, Tena had left the land of her birth.

On board, Tena found to her surprise that there were 53 cards and letters waiting for her, along with two bouquets of flowers, and four packages, all from friends. The gifts and best wishes carried her enthusiasm for a couple of days until March 2 when the sea began to get rough. She started to feel a bit funny and the carefully prepared meals lost their appeal to her. By the next day, the sea was worse and she was so sick that she couldn't even get out of bed. In addition to her seasickness, she also felt homesick and she found herself drawing strength once again from

Psalm 32:8, trusting that the Lord would guide her through the storm with his eyes. By March 6, she was feeling better again, heartened both by the calmer waters on which the SS *Scythia* floated, and by the daily gifts and notes of encouragement she opened from her family.

On March 9, Tena arrived in Liverpool, only to set sail again the following day on the SS *Apapa* of the Elder Dempster line. She was soon seasick again, and the water in the Bay of Biscay was so rough that she didn't dare take off her outer clothing when she went to bed for fear that the ship might go down. The weather soon cleared however and she was able to enjoy the awesomeness of the ocean over the next several days. The sunsets were also beautiful, and they provoked her to write in her travel log, "One is astonished at the beauty of God's creation."

Sitting in her cabin on the eve of March 22, Tena remembered how 24 years ago that day her mother had died. It was from her eternal home that Altje Huizenga would see her only daughter dock the next day along the gold coast of Africa in Takoradi, Ghana.

CHAPTER 5

First Impressions

On March 23, 1937, Tena got her first glimpse of African life. With her excitement nearly at its peak, she and the other passengers spent the day in harbor at Takoradi, Ghana. On the dock, she was intrigued by some of the dissimilarities with American culture. Amused, she took several pictures of the African women, carrying their babies on their backs and carrying heavy loads on their heads, leaving their hands free to talk.

The next stop was Lagos, the coastal capital of Nigeria. It was there that Tena first made note of the African moon in her diary. She wrote, "The moon shone in all its beauty this evening, casting her silver rays upon the water." The moon would continue to fascinate her the entire time she served in Nigeria. Later, when she was on the field at Lupwe, she and Jennie would hold a contest each month to see who could see the new moon first and then, for several days after its arrival, they would enjoy cool evenings on the lawn, reading by its soft light. In July of 1938, she wrote to the family at home,

> When I see the moon shine, as it never does in the northern latitudes, I sometimes feel sorry for you, seeing you do miss much that nature has in store for her children.

From Lagos, still some 900 miles to the southwest of Lupwe, it was off to Port Harcourt, 40 miles up the Niger River into the heart of Nigeria. The evening of March 27, after they had disembarked, she slept in a mosquito net for the first time, an experience which would become a required way of life while she served in Nigeria. The next day, a Sunday, Tena was able to attend her first native worship service.

> I went to a native service and the church was filled to capacity. How inspiring it really was to see these people sing of the resurrection of Christ! Truly the Lord is blessing the work of the mission.

On March 29, the second last leg of her journey was to begin. On the train through the Nigerian interior between Port Harcourt and Makurdi, she was the only white woman on board. All along the way, she freely handed out candies to the young, naked children who rode with her, but inside she was longing to feed their hearts with food of a more spiritual nature. After a visit with some missionaries at Makurdi on the 30th, she finally started the 140 mile trip south to Lupwe early on the morning of March 31. Traveling in the side-car of a motorcycle driven by her new colleague Ed Smith, they stopped a few times along the way in places like Takum where they met the tribal chief as well as some of the local Christians. Despite their brief respites, they arrived at their final destination by noon. Lupwe ... at last! EBENEZER is penned across the top of Tena's diary entry that day. A place-name from 1 Samuel 7:12, Ebenezer means "Thus far has the Lord helped us."

At one point in time, Lupwe had been a walled town but, in 1916, its occupants had moved to Takum, four miles to the north. Takum was a native town of about 3,000 people, but in the surrounding area that would later become part of the mission field, there were another 75,000 natives living in villages and the bush. In 1919, the SUM decided to build a mission station within the walls of the deserted town of Lupwe. Its decision was part of a master plan to erect Christian mission outposts all across the Sudan in an attempt to spread the good news of the gospel of Jesus Christ and to halt the advance of Islam into central Africa.

Tena's first Nigerian worship service would have been in
a church similar to this one in Kwambai.

Situated in the foothills of the Cameroon Mountains, there
was a good spring of water near Lupwe, and the distance from
Takum would be important for health reasons. In the 1920's,
nothing remained of the old "town," except parts of the
surrounding wall. For the most part, the rest had been covered
with mild tropical growth. There were still some healthy locust
bean trees on the five acre compound and these, along with the 30
or so palm trees that adorned the site, gave a pleasant appearance
to the area. While the administrative, medical, and educational
work of the mission would be carried on from Lupwe, Takum
would become pivotal ecclesiastically. The missionaries would
travel there several times a week by bicycle and the gradual
organization of the church and consistory took place. When people
in the surrounding villages became believers, it was the Takum
church of which they would become members.

When Tena arrived at the Lupwe compound, the reception
was grand. She was overwhelmed by all the natives who came out
to see the new "Baturiya," or "white woman." Her colleagues, Ed
and Nelle Smith and Jennie Stielstra, prepared a special dinner to
share with her. She was delighted to find that Nelle and Jennie
had fixed up her hut to be "as cozy as can be." The excitement of
the day was hard to swallow; it was not until the wee hours of the
morning that she was finally able to fall asleep.

Ed Smith standing alongside the motorcycle and side car
that brought Tena to Lupwe.

The festivities were brought to an abrupt halt the next day. It
was time for the newest missionary at Lupwe to get to work. Early
in the morning, Jennie began some preliminary Hausa instruction
for Tena. Hausa was the language of trade throughout the entire
Sudan. A language that linguists say excels in simplicity, elegance,
and wealth of vocabulary, it was the tongue of some four million
Africans living in the area bound by the Sahara Desert on the
north, the Lake Chad regions on the east, the Benue water parting
on the south, and the Niger River on the west. Since it was not
understood by all natives, later Tena would frequently work
through an interpreter who understood both Hausa and the local
dialect.

Her study of Hausa remained high on her agenda for some
time, and there were many points of frustration along the way.
After the first week of study, she wrote in her diary, "I could not
get the 'Suka' tense and became quite discouraged. I felt like
weeping." Nevertheless, by December of that year, she was able to
start reading her Hausa Bible. By the following December, 1938,
she was choosing between two topics on which to write a sermon
in the Hausa language as part of her final Hausa exam. She chose,

"A Woman—A Sinner—Kissed His Feet." On January 6, 1939, she passed the grueling 9 1/2 hour exam, pending completion of her sermon. She finally finished the sermon on February 10, 1939. Exhausted after having worked on it all day, she penned in her diary, "It truly was written in weakness, but as I've done my best, that is all I can do."

When Tena first arrived on the field, she worked with three other missionary colleagues. Ed and Nelle Smith, with their child Alyce Jean (*left*) and Jennie Stielstra, pictured with Nelle Smith (*right*).

In addition to her language study, the first few weeks on the field continued to bring Tena new impressions and experiences. Dress codes were certainly different than they had been in America! At one point, Tena noted how funny it looked that the boys wore their shirts untucked from their shorts. She was surprised, too, at how the natives dressed to attend church. On Sunday, April 25, she traveled to the church at Takum and wrote, "Some of the men had such loose flowing robes, while the women were dressed in gayly colored shawls with some having [turbans] on their heads." Reflecting on the day's activities that had

Map of Nigeria showing location of mission area

concluded with a walk in the moonlight with Jennie, Tena wrote, "How different these Sundays are from those spent at home!"

The following Sunday, May 2, also brought some new experiences. When native couples turned their lives over to Christ, they would often have a ceremony in the church to confirm before God the wedding vows they had previously made as non-believers. Witnessing such a rite, Tena recorded.

It was an outstanding day today. Three men made confession of faith in the midst of the congregation. [Then] Agyu and Naomi ... had their marriage confirmed. They had to wait until the end of the service

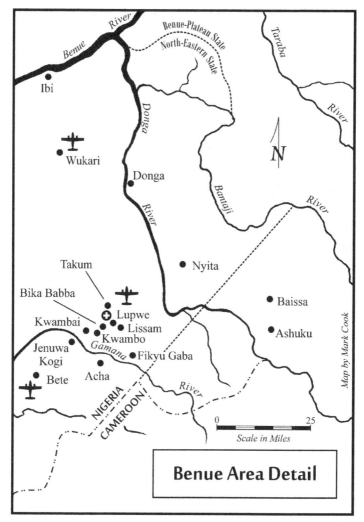

Map of Nigeria, Benue Area Detail

to do this because the bridesmaid came in late for the service. She had her baby on her hip through the ceremony but in the midst of the procedure the baby started to cry, so she had him transferred to her back and tied him with her shawl. Auga and Naomi's baby was also dedicated. How splendid to see such a service!

The next day, Tena was to experience yet another first, but this event would be of a radically different nature. While she held it in her arms, a tiny baby would breathe its last breath. After the service that day, the infant had been brought to the dispensary. Its mother had died and now, with no one to feed it, the baby had developed a bad case of dysentery. The next morning, May 3, the child died. Tena's diary reads,

> I tried to resuscitate it but it did not help. The father himself helped to dig the grave about a half hour after the baby died. I wrapped it up with bandages and later the child was carried to the grave by Isaiah. Ika spoke a few words and prayed at the grave. The parents being Christians, [the baby] was buried in the Christian cemetery.

This young child's passing was only the first of many deaths that Tena would face in her medical work.

CHAPTER 6

Hurting, Healing, and Helping

Over the weeks ahead, as her trunks began to arrive one by one in Lupwe, Tena began to settle into the compound that would become both her home and the focal point for her service to God for 17 years. Her most significant contribution to the everyday work life of the mission would be her nursing knowledge and skills.

The medical work at Lupwe had begun very slowly. In 1921, an average of only 20 patients a month were treated at Lupwe by Johanna Veenstra and Clara Haigh. Although these women had no formal training in nursing, the number of patients treated had risen slowly to 44 per month by 1930. Due to the power and position of witch doctors in the tribal communities, winning the

A group of patients in front of the dispensary in 1937.

confidence of the natives around Lupwe was initially an excruciating process. With each person healed, however, a certain degree of suspicion and distrust was broken.

The first full year under the control of a registered nurse was in 1933 when Bertha Zagers, along with Jennie Stielstra, joined Nelle Breen at the mission. With Miss Zagers setting the course for a fuller medical ministry, the number of new patients treated each month rose sharply to 110. Bertha was able to work out of a primitive dispensary which had been erected at Lupwe for her work. The patients that had traveled long distances and needed extended treatment were able to stay in small huts with simple rooms. She also began the treatment of lepers, a ministry which would continue throughout Tena's term on the field.

A young boy with yaws

Bertha had been gone from Lupwe for about a year when Tena arrived and it became her task to carry on the work that Bertha had begun. Tena, assisted by some Nigerian nurses' aides that she helped train, served as the only registered nurse on the field until 1941 when another nurse, Anita Vissia from Grand Rapids, Michigan, joined the missionary staff. Anita worked with Tena in the dispensary for her first three months at Lupwe but soon began to specialize in leprosy work and pediatrics, freeing Tena to work with the patients who visited the dispensary. Although these two were joined by another registered nurse in 1946, it was not until Tena's final few months on the field that a doctor finally joined the Lupwe medical ranks.

Under Tena and Anita's leadership, the medical mission continued to grow. In 1943, they provided 2,947 patients with 25,824 treatments over the course of the year. Ten years later, the work had almost doubled. In the final six months of 1953, just prior to Tena's returning to America for the last time, the small staff at Lupwe gave over 24,000 treatments. Five years later, the mission opened its own hospital in Takum on November 12, 1958, and the frontier dispensary at Lupwe was closed.

Tena's first exposure to the dispensary was the day after arriving at Lupwe. Right from the beginning, she was to encounter many unusual and difficult cases. She often found herself praying to God, the "Great Physician," for the necessary wisdom and patience to do her job faithfully. It took real fortitude to deal with some of the more unsightly cases. One day in June, 1937, she was called upon to help a man who had traveled three days to the mission with an arm covered in skin ulcers, a girl whose nose was being eaten away with syphilis, and a man who had leprosy so bad that his arms and feet had simply rotted away.

Eye infections, social diseases like yaws, and severe diarrhea were all very common. The list below, indicating the cases treated in 1937, gives an example of the type and variety of sicknesses that Tena was called upon to treat over the course of a year:

Sickness	Cases	Sickness	Cases
[Skin] Ulcers	493	Dysentery	26
Eye cases	130	Accidents	12
Ear cases	80	Backaches	15
Burn cases	31	Breast abscesses	10
Syphilis	576	Hernia	8
Yaws	1100	Hemorrhages	23
Influenza	30	Pneumonia	25
Malaria	72	Abscesses	53
Colds	131	Worm cases	22
Abdominal disorders	150	Fevers	23
Anemia	162	Broken bones	1
Heart trouble	27	Dog bites	2
Headaches	28	Jaundice	3
Throat disorders	3	Bruises	18
Teeth extractions	41	Rheumatism	7
Thyroid	103	Leprosy	166

Besides these ongoing problems, there were also frequent outbreaks of sleeping sickness, smallpox, and cerebral meningitis. These were frightening diseases; the latter two were very contagious and the death rate for all three was high. Writing about a meningitis epidemic in her Medical Report of 1945, Tena wrote,

> For two months of the year, our compound was considered an isolation camp, for large numbers of Cerebral Meningitis Cases were treated on the compound. In all we took care of 73 cases and as we had no isolation ward, we used the leper building, because that had a cement floor. This epidemic lasted from February to the end of March. As this is a new disease in our district, the natives knew no cure for it and were very much afraid of contracting the disease. It was called the white man's disease, for apparently only the white man knew the cure: namely, the magic needle as it is called. Thirteen of this number lie buried in Lupwe's cemetery. Yet, through this entire epidemic no one at Lupwe was smitten with the disease. Needless to say, fear filled their hearts and many times they came to us, asking us for advice regarding the matter. We did rope off the medical area and forbade everyone who had anything to do with the sick to go beyond their own area. God watched over us for which we cannot be thankful enough. At present another epidemic is pending but we have built a crude isolation building off the compound and the sick are cared for there.

For the smallpox epidemics, grass shelters had to be built apart from the mission station and there, the relatives could stay with patients while they required treatment. Sometimes, out of fear, the relatives would abandon their sick kin, making the digging of graves and burial a major problem. Nevertheless, the scare over smallpox helped to promote vaccination. Year after year, Tena and the other Lupwe missionaries would themselves stand in line to be revaccinated in order to assure those who were wary of the procedure that it was safe.

Such an array of medical challenges, typically faced with only the most simple medicines and techniques, often required both creativity and ingenuity. Nonetheless, Tena was always thankful that such basic treatments were able to help so many thousands with difficult and often painful problems. It was a delight, for instance, to see bodies completely covered in ulcers healed after only three weeks of simple treatment.

The prenatal and natal care she was able to provide was particularly satisfying for her, and perhaps the most appreciated by the natives, many of whom had lost several children to death. Some of the mothers, though, had their own ideas about caring for their young ones and Tena had to be patient in teaching them about the importance of hygiene to their children's health. On September 8, 1938, Tena wrote to her brother Pete and his wife Betty:

A sleeping sickness patient at Lupwe.

I am caring for a little babe, who I have named Wilhelmina, for she was born on the queen [of Holland's] birthday. At first the mother let me bathe her without saying anything and the whole dispensary would watch me give her her bath. To care for the cord was one of the most important tasks of the bath, but I could hear the mother mutter each time I tied a binder on the child. Just what she said I could not hear, but it was something that she did not approve of anyway, so this morning when I saw that the binder had been loosened I asked the interpreter why she did not like it, and then she replied that the sore was healed and it no longer needed a covering.

She was also often called upon to care for babies whose mothers had died in delivery. During the day, there were usually native women who could provide milk, but at night it was often necessary for Tena to feed the child with some form of substitute breast milk. After trying carnation milk, late in 1938 she wrote the Tuskegee Institute in Alabama to see if they could provide her with a recipe for a more nourishing emulsion for infants. G. W. Carver, the Director of Agricultural Research, sent back directions for making soybean milk, which could be made just as easily with ground peanuts in place of the soybeans if necessary.

Soybean Milk

Take finely ground soybeans, mix with about 10 parts water; heat slowly to nearly the boiling point for fifteen minutes (stirring frequently). Let stand until the residue settles, or strain through a moderately thick cloth.

With orange, lemon, or fruit juices this milk is extremely palatable, and very nourishing, the milk having an approximate composition of 3.7% protein, 2.0% fat; 1.8% carbohydrates; and 0.5% mineral salts.

The work was often exhausting, not only because the hours were long and the numbers of patients often great but also because the work was sometimes physically demanding. This was especially true of the dental work. Working from a stool, with old dental tools sent from America, and without anesthesia, the work often required strength and dexterity. Tena wrote in her diary on October 27, 1937,

This morning I extracted two [more] teeth which makes the number 23 in all. I sometimes wonder who suffers the most, the patient or I. These were so difficult that [if I could've] I would gladly have avoided taking them out.

Tena knew what it was like to be on the patient's end of this procedure as well. In 1943, she asked her colleague at Lupwe, Ed

Smith, to pull two bad teeth for her. He struggled with the offending oral ivories until he was drenched with sweat, but to no avail. He suggested that they take a break and try again later. Although Tena endured the procedure like a "brick," neither attempts to remove the eye teeth were successful. She had to travel to the hospital at Makurdi to have them removed by Dr. Fox but, even there, no anesthesia was used.

Despite the work's irregularities, Tena tried to establish a routine for her work and the dispensary. At 6:00 A.M., she joined with the school teachers, Bible students, houseboys, nurses' aides, and other missionaries at the Veenstra Memorial Chapel for morning devotions in Hausa. They would sing together and ask God to strengthen them for the work, and to bless the gospel as it was lived out and spoken by the mission staff that day. By 6:30, she was in the dispensary to prepare for the day's challenges and to do some training and planning with her staff of two to three native helpers. It would then be time to gather together the patients who were staying in huts at the mission receiving ongoing treatment of one kind or another. By seven or eight o'clock, depending to a degree on the weather, these patients would join in prayer and song at a small chapel service led by Tena or one of the native nurses' aides like Audu Siman or Yakabu Bete. She would

A patient in front of the huts used for those staying at Lupwe to receive ongoing care.

then check on their condition and provide more medicine if necessary.

After breakfast, it was back to the dispensary to see new patients who had arrived on the compound that day for treatment.

Hopefully by 1:00 P.M., she would have the opportunity to break for lunch and a siesta. The afternoon could be spent in a variety of ways, including Hausa study, more work at the dispensary, women's Bible studies, visiting nearby villages, and, of course, catering to the inevitable emergencies.

By modern standards, the dispensary was a crude structure. Her work there was often interrupted by both small

A patient brought to the dispensary by friends.

inconveniences and major catastrophes. In January of 1939, Tena wrote home to Pete, explaining how Ed Smith and a carpenter were busy at work trying to repair the dispensary walls that had been eaten away by termites. Later, in June 1942, an entire section of the dispensary caved in as the foundation gave way under the heavy rains of the wet season. The worst accident, however, was on October 29, 1951, when lightning hit the dispensary. The resulting fire consumed not only the building but also all the medicines and equipment as well. The medical staff's flexibility and adaptability were tested until a new facility was completed the following year.

Not all of Tena's medical work was to be carried on from the confines of the dispensary, however. Every several months, or whenever conditions allowed, she would have the opportunity to travel to the surrounding villages on a "trek." Outfitted with a limited supply of medicine and equipment, and working from a wobbly table under the shade of a tree, she was able to provide basic health care for those who, for a variety of reasons, could not come to Lupwe for treatment.

Although travel was difficult and, at times, even dangerous, Tena always considered trekking to be one of the most favorite aspects of her work. Her first trek began just after having been on the field for two months. From May 27, 1937, to June 18, she traveled with Jennie to a number of towns and villages on their way to Wukari. After having struck out on bicycles the first day at 6:30 A.M., Tena wrote in her diary later that day,

> We rested at a small place and bought some mangos. Did that ever go good. We arrived at Chan-Chan-Ji at 11:30 A.M. The three cyclists were with us but we had to wait for the other boys who had our chairs and provisions. The chief did not know of our coming, yet he brought us some eggs, limes, and two chickens. A dish of hot pot tasted good and after dinner I felt a lot better.

On Friday, May 28, they were off early again.

> Left for Donga this A.M. at 6:30. Our legs seemed so heavy [at] the beginning of the journey, but before long it became better. The [14 mile] road from Chan-Chan-Ji to Wukari is hilly and we often had to get off our bicycles and walk the hills. We had five cyclists carry our loads and four head carriers. The road leading to Donga was good ... It seems so very hot here and the ground is also very damp.

On this first trek, Tena spent much time in Hausa study under the direction of a native Muslim teacher in Wukari, and also learned much about native customs. She and Jennie also joined in worship and prayer with the local Christians, and took time to share the gospel with the local children. On Monday May 31, she wrote.

> This morning the market children came and asked whether they could have school on the verandah. Jennie promised them a story for this afternoon. About 15 came and the story of Joseph was told in part. After that we played games with them. Putting a bell on one and blindfolding the other, and then letting the blindfolded one catch the other. A great crowd gathered not only of

children but also of [others] who peered through the gate and fence.

Travel was not only by bicycle. On future treks, bringing her small medicine box with her, Tena would also travel on the compound's motorcycle or, when it was available, in an old side car. Many of the treks, however, were through the bush on narrow paths, and travel by foot was the most common. Tena describes one of these trips in her July 23, 1937 diary entry.

We left for Kuambai at 7:00 A.M., walking through the bush path. The grass was so tall that we had to make a way through it. We crossed several bridges and on one of them I slipped and fell into the pond. What a mess I was when I got up! A little further on we came to a pond without a bridge and had to be carried over by the boys. Jennie took a movie picture of this scene which no doubt will be good when seen. Later we crossed another pond and while the boys carried me, they slipped and we fell on top of each other into the water. We were saturated and on top of this it started to rain and we walked through this for a few miles. We were glad to get home and get dry clothes on.

Even when traveling by the motorcycle or car, one was often faced with very poor roads. On one journey, the conditions were so bad that they had to leave the road and drive through the grass. The car hit a rock that was concealed in the brush and the front axle snapped. On another occasion, this same car ended up in the Katsina River and it took two hundred men to haul it out! The travel associated with trekking was not the only difficulty experienced in Tena's medical work. Sometimes new government regulations would temporarily limit the type of care she could provide. As stricter legislation was developed concerning the dispensing of drugs and the giving of injections, the work of the mission would be temporarily curtailed until the nursing staff could obtain permits. Throughout some of the summer and early fall of 1938, for instance, work at the dispensary came almost to a standstill while Tena waited to get a new injection permit. It was a frustrating several months for her with many agonizing moments. The mission was not even permitted to give injections for the dreaded sleeping sickness. People would come with other illnesses as well and, even though the medicine was right at hand, Tena was unable to administer it on account of the new law. Fortunately, for some ailments like snake bites, there was medicine available that could be taken orally.

Crossing Donga River during trekking outing

Perhaps the greatest difficulty in the work, however, was that despite the thousands of successful treatments, there were still many deaths to face. Often the natives would first approach the medicine man or employ pagan rituals in an attempt to bring about healing and only come to the mission as a last resort. As a result, it was often too late to provide any help. On February 23, 1939, Tena wrote,

> A child was brought into the dispensary today while we were at prayers. We did all we could but about 30 minutes later she gasped and was gone. The mother had done "tsafi" for the child with no help. She had cooked [food to the idols] but the idols did not help her, so as a last resort she came to us but alas it was too late.

In another case, Tena tells of a mother who, being urged on by another woman, brought her son of approximately five years to the dispensary in critical condition. The boy weighed only 12 pounds and what little flesh he had was rotting away. When Tena washed out his dirty mouth, five teeth fell out. This boy, too, was soon to be lost.

There were also many others. In a letter to the family on November 26, 1937, she recounted the story of a woman who was doing well but then suddenly died.

This evening I am still under the impression of the death that occurred here this P.M. I'll write you the story so that you can understand the situation. A woman came to us very sick with Pneumonia, which she contracted on the way to us (she lives about 16 miles from us). She had her baby of 2 weeks, weighing just 5 pounds on her back. We treated her and she was convalescing nicely, even sitting outside in the sun in our rest chair. But she got worse and today, surrounded by friends, she went to be with the Lord, we hope. She wanted to follow the Jesus Road, but was beaten by her husband each time. She attended church [but] at last even the Christians in her town suggested that she should remain home, seeing she was hit each time. But it gave her no peace, and when she felt sick she came to us alone, for her husband refused to go with her and would not have anything to do with her. While she was sick the women in the compound took turns nursing the wee little one. At times when I would find it crying I would take it to a nursing mother for a [feeding]. Because she was so tiny I made a little flannel gown for the babe, but she also wore the "tail of a deer." Upon questioning I found out that on the day the child was born the men had caught a deer and seeing the babe could not eat the meat, she got the tail to go around her hips. My heart goes out to some of these people, for they are as human as we, and sometimes even more sensitive. As we stood around the grave I saw them place the woman on a mat, and she was wrapped in an old blue uniform of mine, which I had given her to use as a covering against the flies. A few banana leaves were placed on top of that and then the earth was placed in the open grave. What is man really, and yet we struggle as long as we can. I had bathed the woman in the morning and as I rubbed camphorated oil on her body I thought of the text James 5:14 and, knowing that human help seemed futile, we prayed together. That text has often puzzled me.

James 5:14, the text that puzzled Tena, reads in the NIV, "Is any one of you sick? He should call the elders of the church to pray over him and anoint him with oil in the name of the Lord." Tena knew that the Lord had the power to heal, and that he delighted in healing, because she saw evidence of that almost everyday in the dispensary. But, nevertheless, the agony of death still faced her often. In some diary entries from 1938, she struggled again with the question of death and concluded that it was a mystery, to be left in God's hands.

October 21: I had been up all night so I slept a little while this A.M. My mind would not dwell on anything but on my woman who is in labor but has stopped having contractions. I gave her quinine this afternoon but that did not help. We have prayed a great deal about this case but are leaving it all in the Lord's hand.

October 22: Oh what a day of activity. This woman from Kuambai did not have contractions all night. I tried castor oil again but with no result. We sent a messenger to Dr. Hollins but he advised to wait until the morning. Kisepukum tried to take the baby from the mother but it was a contracted pelvis. As a last resort we took her to Wukari. Kisepukum went with Ed and they stopped at Kufe to consult Dr. Hollins. All was well then but 4 miles later Ed noticed she was unconscious. She swallowed the brandy and he took her back to Kufe. There they worked on her but she died while the doctor was working with her. Ed then brought her home with him and by that time it was about 4:30 P.M. God's ways are different from our ways.

October 23: This morning the mother and father came of Adiza. Oh, how pitiful it was to see them weep. The mother pointed with one finger as if to say, "She was my only child, or daughter." We wrapped her in an old dress of Nelle's and thus entrusted her to the earth. We know not the reason of this but some day we shall understand.

Despite the fact that she was always surrounded by death, Tena never became hardened to it. She always remained compassionate and involved in the lives of her patients, caring for them with tenderness from the heart. Through the struggles and suffering, she never got to the point of despair because she knew she served a God who had conquered death through his son, Jesus Christ.

Tena's house in Lupwe

CHAPTER 7

A *"Vastigheid"* Faith

Tena's hands bathed wounds and gave needles during the day but, at night, they were often folded together as she prayed for her patients. She lifted prayers heavenward for healing, but she also recognized that the needs of her patients often extended beyond the physical. While Tena loved her medical work dearly, she also longed that others might experience the blessings of faith and salvation in Jesus Christ. She concluded her 1946 Medical Report with this prayer.

> May we not only minister to the sick bodies that are entrusted to our care but may we lead them to the Great Physician, who can heal both soul and body.

The God that Tena had come to Nigeria to serve was one in which she laid her entire trust. She could see his hand at work in both the joys and the struggles of life on the mission field. In times of uncertainty, illness, danger, or difficulty, she would often still write in her diary that she was resting in the "Lord's doings," and trusting in him to protect, provide, and work all things together for her ultimate good.

It wasn't always in grandiose ways that she expected him to act. She trusted he was at work even in the daily routine, providing her with energy and help when needed. In her diary on November 1, 1937, she wrote,

Both Jennie and I are busy with the routine duties and are happy in doing the little things, praying that the Lord's blessing may be in the little things which we do.

Throughout her life, she found him to be faithful in those little things but, periodically, she experienced his love and protection in big ways as well. These more dramatic expressions of God's care often came when Tena was traveling through the war years. One of those occasions was on her voyage back to Lupwe after her first furlough. On March 11, 1940, she wrote to Jennie in Lupwe, "I do hope nothing will hinder me from sailing, but should hindrances come I must be patient, believing that in the Lord's own appointed time I will be in your midst." On March 30, Tena sailed from New York on the SS *Conte Di Savoia* of the Italian Line for Genoa, Italy, arriving there on April 10. Nineteen days later she sailed on the SS *Sistiana* from Genoa and arrived in Lagos, Nigeria, on May 27. The day after she landed in Africa, Italy entered the war against Britain and normal communications were cut off.

Again in 1943, Tena found herself trusting in God for her safety as she headed for home to begin her second furlough. On April 6, she boarded an American freighter, the SS *Zarembo*, at Lagos. On the first leg of the journey to Takoradi, they were spotted by enemy aircraft and the gunmen on board had to take their positions. Nevertheless, they arrived at Takoradi on April 9 and sailed from there on April 26 with 18 other ships and four escorts. On April 29 her ship left the convoy to go to Marshall. Describing the events that followed, Tena wrote in her travel log.

Seven hours after we left the convoy, a submarine attacked the commodore's ship and every one on board was lost. The ship that took our position and the ship next to us were torpedoed and seven ships in all were sunk. Praise the Lord we were kept in safety.

Later in the journey, Tena wrote a letter to Jennie from on board:

The Lord has given us quietness and peace of mind thus far. None of us are over anxious and each day we come together in the morning and in the evening for a time of Bible study. Many precious promises are being claimed as ours during the journey and we are praising Him for the peace of mind that is ours as we sail through these troubled waters.

The steadfast trust through all circumstances that Tena placed in God likely arose out of the experiences she enjoyed of his presence. Describing one of those experiences in her diary on June 13, 1937, she wrote,

We climbed the incline this afternoon and sat on top of the hill reading a sermon once given at Keswick, England. I certainly was inspired and felt I had been the Lord, apart from the world, and [I] could come down again better fitted for the task before me.

Again, on May 19, 1942, she could write to Jennie,

The Lord has been wonderfully near to me these days. I have enjoyed His presence in a remarkable way of late and I rejoice to know that I am His and He is mine. I have had some wonderful times with the Lord on the rocks round about Miango.

As at Miango, it was often times in the out of doors where Tena experienced God. She frequently wrote of "the handiwork" of God in nature, and of "all nature proclaiming the glory of God." She experienced God in other ways too, however. Celebrating communion was always a particularly meaningful time for her. As she knelt to receive the elements of bread and wine, she often marveled at how, in Christ, God had made her one with the natives she lived amongst. On New Year's Eve, 1938, she found herself writing home to the family,

Tomorrow we hope to have a communion service and then about 30 will sit with us at the Lord's table. It surely is wonderful how race and color is forgotten here, and the oneness in Christ is felt.

Tena at Lupwe

Tena lived a life of gratitude, often "counting" her many daily blessings. Among other things, she regularly thanked God for his leading in her life, for progress in the mission work, for the prayer and financial support of churches back home, for health and safety, and, importantly, for friends and family.

This attitude of thanksgiving affected her entire character. It provided her with a joy within that allowed her to be truly joyful in her daily living as well. She was almost always close to laughter, and her gregarious nature allowed her good sense of humor to arise often, as it did in May 1937. With Ed and Nelle Smith ready to leave on furlough, Tena took their night clothes, knotted them, and then hid them from the would-be travelers!

This zest for life usually carried over into celebrations as well. Tena made sure that everyone's birthday and all the holidays were enjoyed in grand style. This, of course, went for her own birthdays too! Writing home to the family on February 28, 1939, she described her 32nd birthday, celebrated just two days previous. Ed had gone up the hill for the weekend to the little mission hut that was used as a quiet place for study and rest. She and the others had promised to join him there for tea so that he wouldn't miss Tena's birthday. In honor of the special day, they enjoyed salmon sandwiches which "seemed to taste better after the climb." The view was beautiful from the hill, with much of the mission district in sight.

> All too soon did that hour pass and we had to go down ... As we were coming down, eight deer could be seen at the bottom of the hill and did the boys get excited when they saw them run.
>
> Then at night we invited the natives to the house and we had a good sing song. About forty were crowded on the verandah and the odor of the many bodies certainly was keenly noticeable. But we got in the spirit of singing and so sang for an hour. We then put on the radio and listened to some peppy German music ... [Later] we had a brief period of prayer and then they all went home ... Then we went to see if Ed was still outside and sure enough we could see his lantern quite plainly, and so I blew my whistle two longs and two shorts which he heard, and the flashing of our lights told one another that we were signaling him. He responded, and it was rather amusing, and jestingly I said, "The boka man of Kunabe will be thinking he has another competitor on our hill." Then we went in and, in comfortable chairs, we listened to a sermon from Ireland which was very good. And when Nelle rang the evening bell telling everyone to go to bed, we had to look whether Ed was still up, and sure enough he was, and when he saw our light he again flashed.

Clearly, Tena loved life, and the Lord who is the giver of life. This love for her Lord was unshakable. Rev. Henry Evenhouse, with whom Tena had grown up at First CRC in Chicago and who became Tena's "boss" in the 1950's, used the term "vastigheid"—

"sturdiness of commitment" or "fastness"—in trying to describe Tena's faith.

CHAPTER 8

Teaching and Preaching

Tena had many opportunities to share the faith that had shaped her so profoundly because, in addition to her medical work, she was also frequently able to teach and preach. Besides the daily opportunity that the chapel services at the dispensary provided, she was also able to spread the good news of Christ at informal gatherings and church services as well.

Her desire to share her faith arose out of a genuine compassion for those whose lives she encountered. In the early days on the field, when her Hausa was still very limited, she longed to communicate with the smiling faces she greeted each day at the dispensary, telling them of the joy she had found in Christ and of the salvation that comes through him alone. But even in those early years, she still had opportunities to pass along her hope in Christ through the means of an interpreter. On December 12, 1937, she recalled in her diary the first occasion in which she addressed a "congregation."

> This morning I arose early to go to a place in back of the hill from here to preach. By some misunderstanding, we went two hours later than we had planned. We went and found a chapel for services and 52 gathered to hear the Old Old Story. Nzugum and Ishaku went with me and for the first time I told the story of Christ's coming through an interpreter.

It would not be until the following fall, however, that Tena would speak in one of the mission's official churches. On October 7, 1938, Tena wrote to Jennie, who was home on furlough, to tell her how the opportunity came about.

> Last Sunday [October 2nd] I preached for the first time. Ed was to have arranged for a preacher from town, but as he was not at home and no preparations were made. At about 7 o'clock on Saturday I called Audu and asked who was going to preach on the morrow, and then he told me that no one had been asked. So then I made preparations and I really got a great joy out of it, as I looked into their eager faces.

In the years that followed, Tena had many opportunities to preach, not only in Lupwe and Takum but also in the surrounding villages like Atsafo and Bika-a-Baya as well. As her Hausa improved, she was also able to serve as an interpreter for visiting English preachers at the mission. Rev. Henry Evenhouse fondly recalls one such time that Tena provided this service for him. In 1947, he and Rev. John DeKorne were visiting the field from the CRC's Foreign Mission Board in Grand Rapids, and he had been asked to preach at four different mission stations surrounding Lupwe on Ascension Day. Using the same sermon, Rev. Evenhouse and Tena endured the long morning, with Tena faithfully interpreting the message at the first three services. At the fourth service, Tena already knew the message quite well and, getting hungry by that point, decided to take matters into her own hands. Midway through the sermon, Rev. Evenhouse elaborated on an important point and waited for Tena's translation to follow. Instead she looked up at him with a smile and told him in English, "I've said that part already. Let's speed things up!"

Besides preaching and interpreting for other preachers, Tena taught Sunday School classes and Bible Studies. Her nieces and nephews would sometimes send their old Sunday School papers from their own church school to Tena and then, using these and other resources, Tena would type out Sunday School lessons and send them to the evangelists for use in the local churches. She marveled at how the gospel message was universal, able to speak to all peoples in all ages. One Sunday, early in her work on the field, she noted how a group of people came around her verandah after Sunday School, asking to see pictures of Jesus on the cross. Some in the group wept as they considered Christ's sacrifice on their behalf. Another Sunday, she was struck by the faith of one of her young Sunday School pupils as he told her how he had tried to tell the men in his village about Jesus.

A group of children gathered in front of Tena's house.

Despite these signs of promise, however, the work of evangelism was also at times discouraging and full of disappointment. In writing to Rev. John DeKorne at the CRC Mission Office in June 9, 1941, Tena noted:

> During April I spent most of my time on the station in the medical work and several times during the week I would cycle into Takum and visit the Hausa compounds. As these Hausa homes are all Mohammedan, the women cannot leave their homes unless they are properly chaperoned. Thus, they rarely ever leave their compounds during the day, and consequently they cannot hear the Gospel. I have been burdened for these women for some time and although it is discouraging

work, I feel that we must tell them the glad news of Salvation. One of the women from Takum usually accompanies me, and I must say that we have had times of spiritual blessing, but then there were also times when I would return home, feeling as though my work of the afternoon had been in vain.

An ongoing source of frustration in the work were the many instances of polygamy, even among those in the church who had professed their faith in Jesus Christ. On several occasions, Tena mourned as another's relationship to the church was severed because they refused to honor the vows of marriage that they had made before God.

Nevertheless, the fact that God changed peoples' lives and the church grew made the preaching and teaching exciting. When Tena was home on furloughs, she used to tell some of these stories of new faith while traveling from church to church doing deputation work. One of her favorites was the story of Astira, a woman who had been lured from her home with a group of other children with some cola nuts and bananas by a band of slave traders. When the British took control in Nigeria, the practice of raiding young children to be sold as slaves in foreign countries became illegal. For many years, river travelers were stopped by police and their belongings and canoes were searched. Children were often found hidden under the mats on the floors of the canoe. However, many of these children had been stolen from distant places and did not know the whereabouts of their villages. Because their parents could not be found, these children were taken to the SUM's Mission orphanage in Wukari. It was in this way that Astira found herself at the orphanage, and it was there that she heard about the Lord Jesus Christ and gave her life to him. It was also there that she met Fillibus and, together, they served as evangelists in Takum for several years. Even though Fillibus died relatively young, Astira remained one of the outstanding women in the church, serving and leading in a variety of capacities.

Tena's teaching among the natives was broad, and included manual skills as well as knowledge about the faith. At different times throughout her Nigerian career, she found herself teaching sewing to women's groups, teaching women in her home how to do various types of handiwork, or simply helping people on her veranda in the evening with knitting projects.

Her concern for the welfare of Nigeria and her people was also broad. At one point, concerned about the status of the women that she lived amongst and worked with, she sent a poem entitled "The African Woman's Plaint" to a missionary magazine to be reprinted. She wrote, "This poem portrays African womanhood, and I feel sure you, too, will pray with me that the day will soon be here when our African woman will be able to feel that she is indeed a companion to her husband."

The African Women's Plaint

A woman's place is lowly
I know and grumble not;
I am one of millions,
And share the common lot;
But sometimes in the darkness dim,
These musings come unsought.

Why is the white man's wife
So different from ours?
Why do they live as equals,
With equal gifts and powers?
The black-skinned husband stands erect,
Abject his woman cowers.

The white man's wife has garments,
But leaves for me are meet.
She counsels with her husband,
But scorn my words would greet.
She sits amid his kinsman all,
I grovel at their feet.

She travels with her husband,
They go with equal tread;
He tries to ease her journey,

I trudge along behind.
A living load behind me hung—
A burden on my head.

He loved, he wooed, he won her;
She freely loved and gave.
My husband gave the cattle—
No more—and I his slave
Was never asked about the love
Now buried in hope's grave.

She eats beside her husband;
I eat in place apart.
'Tis true, these are our customs.
But something in my heart
Cries, "Why should she be honored so,
And I am made to smart?"

I've heard, "In long ages
Her lot was just like mine,
Until One came to raise her—
One human, yet divine."
I wonder if He'll come to me and if
He'll alter mine.

CHAPTER 9

Irritating Insects and Ominous Obstacles

All of Tena's work—the medical, the preaching and teaching, the concern for social issues—was met by significant challenges and, at times, faced serious difficulties. The natural environment itself placed a whole host of demands on those who entered the land as a foreigner. The first full month that Tena spent in Lupwe, May 1937, she kept a record of the temperature in her diary. A third of the days in that month saw temperatures between 110 and 120 degrees, while another third saw the thermometer register between 100 and 110. These temperatures, coupled with extreme humidity, especially in the wet season, often made for taxing work conditions and restless nights of sleep.

The animals and insects also posed a constant threat. Cape Buffalo, crocodiles, and hippos were a remote but nonetheless real hazard. A more imminent concern were the scorpion sting and the snake bite, both of which were common and potentially deadly. But the most common danger of all was that posed by the ever-present insects. The mosquito and the tsetse fly, as notorious disease carriers, were particularly dreaded. Although medicines for the prevention and treatment of malaria improved over the course of Tena's term on the field, she nevertheless was struck by the illness many times. In September of 1938, she struggled with a particularly bad case of it. At one point, her temperature rose to 104.2 degrees and she felt "as meek as a lamb." She was so weak that she couldn't address an envelope for a letter that was waiting to be sent home. The only medicine for malaria in those early days was quinine and she was forced to take it in such large doses that she could scarcely hear anyone talking because her ears were ringing so loudly. Her appetite left her and, after living on a liquid diet for two weeks, she lost 10 pounds from her ordinarily robust frame. When the fever lifted, she would feel fine and, with her work constantly beckoning her, she would be back in the dispensary greeting her patients. The exertion, however, would typically put her back in bed the following day. Finally, after several weeks of erratic fever and sickness, she was on her feet again.

Whereas the mosquito and tsetse fly posed health threats, insects like the common bee and fly were a constant nuisance. On December 31, 1938, she wrote home to the family.

> Since yesterday I have been troubled with bees in my bathroom. They were in the bathroom primarily but some escaped into the bedroom and verandah. A few minutes ago I called [one of the native helpers and asked if he would] burn straw in order to get rid of them. He said, "Baturiya, you must have something sweet in your bathroom, otherwise they would not come there." I said, "What could attract them in the bathroom, there is no food here." Yet he insisted that there must be something so he opened the little cabinet in which I keep my creams and a few medicines and believe it or not in the corner there was a hive of bees. We are therefore leaving it until it is dark and then he will take the cabinet out and if possible burn the bees. It must be done in the dark or else they will sting us to such an extent that nothing can be done about it. This noon I scarcely dared to take my bath for fear I might get stung but I was reassured that if I let them alone they would leave me alone. I tried to leave them alone but alas I was stung three times. Ah, such is life!

Tena's health problems on the field also included tropical leg ulcers. They began as early as her first few months on the field and recurred throughout her seventeen year ministry. They could become quite painful and, at times, walking became extremely difficult and possible only with a cane. In 1953 and the early months of 1954, the ulcers became relentless and, eventually, they drove her from Lupwe to America for the last time.

In addition to these difficulties of climate and disease, an entirely different set of challenges faced Tena and the other missionaries as a result of WWII. Contact with family at home became very limited. Many letters between Chicago and Lupwe were sunk at sea and the ones that made it through were often greatly delayed. It was not unusual for Tena to go for 12 week stretches at a time without any word from home.

Letters were not the only thing scarce during the War. Shortages were many and rationing became a way of life. Even basics like butter and sugar became hard to obtain and Tena and the Lupwe team relied on friends and family all over Africa and Europe to provide them with items of varying kinds. "Live on the country" became a common slogan and the missionaries were provided with books containing recipes on how this might be possible. The small garden at Lupwe that was a leisurely hobby previous to the War became an important necessity. The insects and deer combined to make crop loss significant, and the alternating wet and dry seasons created yet another set of unique challenges to gardening. While the small plot rarely flourished, it nevertheless provided an ample supply of sundry vegetables. Lettuce, pumpkins, melons, corn, lima beans, radishes, and cucumber were all enjoyed from the garden. The fruit trees on the compound were typically more reliable and oranges, custard apples, guavas, mangos, and bananas kept Tena busy canning.

Tomatoes were also grown in the garden, but Tena had never developed a taste for them before coming to Nigeria. She was jealous, however, of the enjoyment that Jennie and the other missionaries seemed to derive from eating them and she eventually made herself try them. She discovered to her amazement that she loved them, and she soon became an avid promoter of the little red fruit. After hearing that Jennie's father didn't like tomatoes, she wrote a short note to him in America telling him how tasty they were and insisting that he try them again. She indulged in her new found love, sometimes slicing up a whole plate of them to enjoy in a single sitting! Her affair with tomatoes, however, was somewhat short-lived for the acid in them made her hands break out into open sores. Tena had to learn the hard way the truth in the old adage, "Moderation in all things!"

There were other shortages as well that the missionary team faced in the War years. Items of almost every shape and size were hard to obtain. Necessity became the mother of invention and Tena learned how to make her own soap using palm oil and white ash from the cooking stove. The shortage of items like rubber for tires and the rations on petrol made travel by bicycle or car almost impossible.

For many of the months of international friction leading up to WWII, Tena had to rely exclusively on her letters from America to hear the developing scenario of military entanglements. When a wind powered generator was installed at Lupwe in mid 1938, however, word of the troubled days approaching could be heard over a radio at the compound. The 120 pound generator was hoisted up the newly built tower early in July. After several failed attempts to raise it to its necessary location at the top, Ed Smith struck on an idea that eventually worked. The generator was tied to an empty tub that was carried to the top of the tower. Forming a human chain up the tower, they handed one another bricks which, when they reached the top, were then placed in the tub. When the right weight had been achieved in the tub, it came down and the generator went up! Later in July, wires were pulled with the motorcycle from one pole to the next. The 4x4 poles had been sawn by natives and circled the compound. After attaching wings to the generator and filling the rechargeable batteries with acid, electric light arrived in Lupwe on August 6, 1938.

At first the natives had been wary of the tower. A rumor circulated that there was a war on and that Ed had built the tower so that he could climb it to see when the soldiers were coming. When he sounded the alert, the missionaries would escape on the motorcycle, leaving all the natives that were free of sleeping sickness to be enlisted in the army. The rumors were dispelled, however, when it became apparent that the tower could generate artificial light and, although at first frightened, they later appreciated the light over their huts in the evening. In a few days, electricity was available in Tena' house and she was able to operate the radio sent for her birthday from the family earlier in the year.

The radio did not always work because there was often not enough wind for the generator to charge the batteries. There were other times when the radio needed replacement parts or when lightning would knock the batteries temporarily out of service, but when the radio was working, the compound gathered around Tena's verandah at 7:00 every evening to hear the news. The radio served to break the isolation that Tena and the others had experienced prior to its inception at Lupwe, and allowed them to follow the developments in the War in the years ahead.

Despite the difficulties of the War years and the frustrations of malaria and tropical ulcers, Tena's biggest struggle on the field was the bouts of loneliness she faced. Although she missed her family from almost her very first day at Lupwe, it was not until over a year later that her tear ducts first burst. She wrote in her diary on June 14, 1938, "I had my first good cry in Africa tonight. I felt very lonely." Three days later, however, she was able to write, "The whole world looks good to me again. The dark clouds seem to have rolled away." But by August 2, the clouds of loneliness were back. She wrote, "This evening I have that lonely feeling coming over me again."

Wind-generated power came to Lupwe in 1938. Ed Smith, atop the tower, works on the generator.

She was to experience that lonely feeling on and off throughout her life at Lupwe. Tena was not a loner. She was at her best when surrounded by a host of people, or when in conversation with a close friend. She found that close companion in Jennie Stielstra. It was when Jennie was away on furlough that Tena felt the pangs of loneliness most acutely. In Jennie, she recognized a "kindred spirit" and she believed their relationship was providential. It was to Jennie that Tena was able to open her heart, sharing both her joys and fears. While Jennie was in America on furlough, Tena wrote her on October 27, 1946,

> I feel in need of a chat with you and I do miss you very very much at times. I thank God that we have understood one another in the past and I shall always think back to the times of fellowship which we have had together, whether it was in trouble or while the sun shone brightly without a cloud on the horizon.

But even Jennie's congenial companionship was not enough to stop Tena from thinking of home and longing to be there. One night in 1942, she even dreamt that she flew home by plane, surprising the entire family with her arrival!

CHAPTER 10

Rest, Renewal, and Recreation

Despite the myriad challenges of serving on a frontier mission post, Tena loved her life in Nigeria and the contribution she was making towards God's advancing kingdom. While the work may have been taxing in many ways, it was also very diverse and the variety kept Tena invigorated and always ready to face the new day.

Life at Lupwe, however, was not "all work and no play." In fact, despite its demands, there was a leisurely quality to life at Lupwe. Tena wrote home on July 20, 1938,

> I know it will be hard to get used to the fast way of things at home [when I eventually return]. We ... are becoming children of nature, and I find that this life has many advantages and joys. I do long for loved ones but I rarely ever get a longing for the busy life which you are having there. I am perfectly content with this quiet life, yes I would say I prefer it.

With the time she had when work was done, Tena developed a number of interests including stamp-collecting, tennis, and reading, in addition to her hobby of gardening.

Stamp-collecting seemed like a natural hobby to develop for one who sent and received so much mail. Tena's brother at home, Pete, was an avid collector and in October of her first year on the field, Tena embarked on the philatelist trail as well. By means of collector's chain letters, she communicated with hobbyists around the world, sending and receiving stamps. Pete kept Tena supplied with stamp hinges and in their ongoing correspondence, they shared collector's tips. Pete was thrilled in 1953 when a letter came from Tena adorned with Nigeria's new coronation stamp.

While stamp-collecting kept Tena busy for many hours indoors, tennis brought her outside for some physical exercise. In the cool of the evening, she would often lob the ball back and forth over the net with one of the other missionaries. One evening, thinking a jump over the net would be sporty, she fell and sprained her ankle, temporarily ending her tennis career!

She also spent many hours enjoying a good book. Much of her reading was on missions and, many a time, she was inspired in her own work by others who had labored for God either in Africa or elsewhere. Johanna Veenstra's books held a special appeal for her, but she was also fascinated by how God was at work in places like Burma and the Orient as well. While she dabbled a bit in theology, she also enjoyed the "racy" *Gone With the Wind*, the *National Geographic*, and the serial stories in the *Saturday Evening Post*.

Perhaps above all these, however, she relished reading denominational materials the most. Tena's relationship with her church, the CRC, was fundamentally wrapped up with her faith. There was no mistaking the fact that she identified herself as a Reformed believer and, although she was never argumentative, she wasn't the least bit timid espousing the principles of that faith whenever they were challenged. She eagerly awaited copies of the denomination's weekly magazine, the *Banner*, to arrive on the field and, even though they were often several months out of date by the time they were received, she often stayed up late reading them from cover to cover. She also followed the decisions of the denomination's largest ruling body, the Synod, through the Agenda and Acts of Synod that were published each summer after that body had met for its annual deliberations. Tena loved to pore over these publications and, at Sunday tea, she enjoyed engaging the other missionaries in conversation concerning the issues of church, Christian school, and missions.

As a consequence of her loyalty and love for the Reformed faith, she welcomed the 1939 synodical decision that resulted in the CRC officially adopting the Lupwe mission field that the SUM had opened 20 years previous. While she was concerned about what changes the decision might bring to the field, she was proud that the church that was her home would now be responsible for her work.

In addition to her reading, Tena was also a prolific writer. She regularly wrote articles for the *Banner, Missionary Monthly*, and the *Instructor*, and some of these were in Dutch. But more than anything else, she wrote volumes and volumes of letters. In her first 10 months on the field, she wrote over 250 letters to family, friends, and supporters. She kept people up-to-date on her work and asked to be kept up-to-date by them on family and local church news. The letters also included "thank-you's" to the scores of church members and church groups back home that faithfully supported her work by sending items like strips of old bed sheets and discarded white shirts for bandages.

There were also periodic opportunities to get away from the dispensary and compound for a time of rest and recuperation. At Jos, located 290 miles north of Lupwe in the Plateau province, the SUM had established a center where missionaries from across the Sudan could come for a brief vacation. It was the spring of 1938 before Tena could make her first trip to the cooler climes of Jos. She found the luxuries of ice cream for dessert, invigorating air, and time for fellowship with other missionaries much to her liking. There was also time for letter writing and reading, for prayer and Bible study, for exchanging recipes and knitting patterns, for Hausa study, and for visiting the nearby hospital in Vom to learn of new medical techniques and procedures. Each trip to the plateau brought her back to the mission restored and better equipped to face the work ahead. While she enjoyed these breaks, it was always nice to get back "home" again to Lupwe. After spending three and a half weeks in Jos, she penned a poem in her diary upon setting foot again in her hut on May 28, 1938,

Home Again

The best part of holidays
Is the coming home;
Happy feet are they that turn
From the world to roam.
Just the first small glimpse you get
Seems to thrill you through
Of your house among the trees
Smiling out at you.

Coming home to plants and things
On the window sill
(Same old row of Poplar trees
There against the hill)
Rooms look kind of cozy
Like at the dusk of day
Seem to think more of the place
Since we've been away.

Coming home to school and work
(Dear old routine things)
Health in every pulsing vein
Seems to move on wings
Dear familiar room and bed
Fireplace and den
Holidays are wonderful
When you're home again.

The missionary rest center at Jos was an important means for Tena to periodically restore her strength. However, the demands upon one's physical and mental health that the work entailed resulted in a policy that sent missionaries on a furlough to their homeland after every two and a half to three years of service on the field.

Tena's first furlough was in the early summer of 1939. She had originally been scheduled to leave in May but her travel plans were delayed until early in June. She was disappointed about the delay as she was eager to see loved ones again, but she had been so well received in Nigeria that many of the natives wished the delay was longer. She wrote to the family on May 3, 1939,

> This morning when I announced [the delay in my travel] to some of my patients, one said that he wished that there was [another] delay. Another one said that the country had received me so well that it would be better if I stayed on another year. Then Jennie tells me that my appetite is so good that there is no need for me to go home ... I am still full of health and pep [and] I have said jestingly that I had better lose some weight and look more tired for [in my present condition] the people at home will also say that it was not necessary for me to come home. I am truly thankful for this health, and I must admit that I feel much better than [even] last year before I went up [to Jos] for my vacation.

Later on in the letter, she expressed her own mixed feelings about leaving.

> I'm telling you, we do have a fine group of people here, and at times, I feel loathe to leave them. If the weather was always as delightful here as it is early in the morning and after five o'clock, this would be an ideal summer resort but alas, the scorching sun makes her presence felt all too keenly. And then this country abounds with insects and every imaginable creeping thing. But on the whole it isn't bad at all, and I have enjoyed my first term.

On June 10, 1939, Tena was aboard the SS *Abasso* setting sail from Port Harcourt for Plymouth, England. She arrived thirteen days later and then crossed the English Channel to visit friends and relatives in Holland for four weeks. She basked in the warmth of her reception there and, many times, she "felt the ties of blood." She then sailed from Southhampton on July 25, 1939, on the SS *Acquitania,* finally arriving back in America at New York on August 1, 1939.

Tena would also have three additional furloughs in the future. Her second furlough saw her leave Nigeria on April 5, 1943. Travel home on the SS *Zarembo* was delayed several times as a result of WWII and it was over two months later on June 11, 1943, that she finally arrived in New York. While furloughs were typically intended to be six or seven months, she was not able to set sail again for Nigeria until August 19, 1944, on account of the War. With fourteen months in America, she did some nursing work in the hospital as well as carried out her regular furlough duties.

On her third furlough, she was able to fly for the first time, leaving Nigeria on an airplane on May 11, 1947. Six months later, she was in the air again en route to Nigeria. Her final furlough was once again via airplane and, after a visit to Italy, Switzerland, and Holland, she arrived in the USA on December 18, 1950. On July 27, 1951, she left for Nigeria for what would be her final term.

In Chicago on furlough, Tena *(fourth from left)* enjoyed the gathering of family around the dinner table.

While home on furloughs, the first few weeks were usually designed as a time of complete rest. Soon, however, her deputation work would begin in earnest and she would travel to churches and schools throughout North America to update the congregations she visited on the work at Lupwe and to develop in the children an interest in Missions. The furlough would typically end with four weeks of vacation.

Tena's outgoing and demonstrative nature made her well suited for deputation work. She wrote in her diary how much she enjoyed meeting so many people and sharing with them the needs of Africa. In the schools, the fifteen-foot python snake skin that she brought with her was always a tremendous hit with the children and she fascinated them with her tales of a "far-off land." She also brought some native costumes with her and she would dress up one of the children and have them assist her in the storytelling. Whenever she visited Chicago schools, it was almost invariably a niece or nephew whom she dressed in the Nigerian garb and they stood proudly beside their Aunt Tena as she told her adventures. She would tell the children about native dress and diet customs, and a little bit about the home and school life of a Nigerian child. After relating some additional things about the Lupwe compound and the work of a missionary, she would challenge the children to help their Christian "cousins" in Africa with prayer, gifts, and acts of service.

Her message varied depending on the group she was speaking to. When addressing a women's meeting, she would often speak of issues pertaining to Nigerian womanhood. After introducing the role of the African woman in home and work life, she would talk about the unique influence that the women were exercising in the Nigerian church. She would also speak of particular problems that the African woman faced, including the difficulties associated with polygamy. She would conclude by encouraging the women to become involved in the work of missions by interesting their children in mission work, providing bandages, supplies, and other types of support, and considering other avenues of ministry.

Her church talks addressed the issues of mission more broadly. She would relate the history of church missions in Africa with an emphasis on the work at Lupwe and the other CRC missions which were established nearby. She told her listeners why it was important that they were trying to build an indigenous church, with the Nigerian people themselves taking leadership and control. Finally, after a look ahead to the future, she would

challenge the congregation to faithfully pray for God's work in the
world.

Her itinerary was often aggressive. On a seven week Western
trip in 1951, she visited the following places:

Wellsburg, IA	At the evening service For the Queen Esther Society
Denver, CO	For the patients at the Sanatorium At the prayer meeting of the Reformed Church Christian High School Elementary School Ladies Aid An evening service in the Second Church
Alamosa, CO	Sunday evening service
Rehoboth, NM	At the High School For the entire group in the afternoon Showing moving pictures in the evening
Zuni, NM	Zuni school
Tucson, AZ	At a luncheon for a group of women At an evening meeting
San Diego, CA	Evening service
Bellflower, CA	Sunday School—Third Church
Glendale, CA	At an evening service
Redlands, CA	Missionary Union Meeting A.M. Movies in the Evening Service
Artesia, CA	Movies and speech, especially for young people

Hanford, CA	Christian School Slides and Speech at an evening service
Alameda, CA	Sunday night service
Modesto, CA	Movies and slides at an evening service
Ripon, CA	Movies and speech at an evening service High School Elementary School
Escalon, CA	Slides at an evening service and speech
Seattle, WA	Sunday Evening Service
Duvall, WA	Sunday Afternoon Service
Sunnyside, WA	Elementary School movies and a speech an evening service
Everett, WA	Slides and a speech at an evening service
Lynden, WA	Slides and speech at an evening service Missionary Union Meeting
Mount Vernon, BC	Missionary Union Meeting
Abbotsford, BC	Sunday Afternoon service
Sumas, WA	Evening service
Vancouver, BC	Slides and a speech at an evening service
Neerlandia, AB	Evening service
Edmonton, AB	Movies and a speech at an evening service
Granum, AB	Message at a Sunday afternoon service

Nobleford, AB	Message at a Sunday Evening service
Iron Springs, AB	A Dutch message at an afternoon meeting
Lethbridge, AB	Slides, movies and a message at evening service
Conrad, MT	Movies and a message at an evening service
Manhattan, MT	Movies and a message at an evening service

Six days later, upon returning to Chicago, another round of deputation work began in Illinois, Iowa, and Michigan. By the end of it all, she had spoken 99 times and slept in 74 different beds.

As much as Tena loved deputation work, however, the best part of her furloughs was being reunited with family. She would stay in a room at the home of her brother Pete and his wife Betty, but from there she would visit all the Huizenga tribe. Sharing meals and laughter together, and celebrating birthdays and holidays together, was a far cry better than relying primarily on the mail to keep the family close.

CHAPTER 11

Love, Long Distance

While Tena's furloughs served as a welcome opportunity to tangibly share in the lives of her kin, most of her love and concern had to be expressed from the opposite side of the ocean. Through her years of service at Lupwe, she worked hard at keeping the family in touch.

Mail day was always the biggest day for Tena at Lupwe because it was then that she would be able to devour with interest the letters she received from home. On July 20, 1938, she wrote to the family,

Mingled feelings always swell up within my breast after the mail has been read. This time you have remembered me well, for I have letters from Ma, Betty, Bertha, Harry and Jean, and one from Pete. How wonderful it really is to be able to read and write letters, for now I can in a measure live along with you, and I hope you with me. Distance

Mai Yaki carried mail to Lupwe on his head once every two weeks.

may divide us but thoughts go hither and yon, and of course in thought I am with you at present.

Tena's delight in receiving letters inspired her to sit down one day with pen in hand and express how she felt about that wonderful tool of communication: the letter.

A letter to me brings a blessing, when it
　comes with its message clear
That message of joy from a Christian, to one
　in Christ, equally near
So please don't forget that a LETTER
　can do what perhaps you can't do
It can cover the distance that you can't
　and in time bring an answer to you.

While Tena and her brother Pete maintained a particularly close relationship through the stacks of letters they exchanged, Tena corresponded with all of the Huizenga family. It wasn't necessarily important news that Tena awaited in the mail, for she even loved to read about the simple routines and little everyday happenings of the family. As a result, when the demands of life on the American side of the Atlantic made family members temporarily unfaithful in their correspondence, Tena was not adverse to writing a scathing letter of rebuke!

Tena's thoughts would turn most often to home on holidays like Thanksgiving and Christmas, or on relatives' birthdays and anniversaries. Like the rest of her family, Tena loved a celebration and it was particularly painful to be away for these important family occasions. October 26, 1937, was the first such party that Tena missed as the Huizengas got together to celebrate the tenth wedding anniversary of Tena's brother Sam and his wife, Bertha. Pete, writing to Tena the day before, noted,

I assure you that we shall miss you tremendously on this our first family get together since your departure. However we shall just pretend that you are right there and think about you often.

Their years apart didn't make any difference in Tena's being missed when the family gathered together. Eleven years later, on December 27, 1948, Pete was still able to write,

> Tomorrow we are all going to Aunt Jen's for a Huizenga reunion. We shall miss you, for it won't really be a reunion unless we're all there.

Tena made sure to at least participate in spirit at each of these gatherings. Her cards, flowers, and gifts made it clear that she was not far from them in thought. Pete, who frequently looked after her gift buying, often wrote that he was astounded by her memory of these special events, and of her diligence in making sure that some form of greeting or best wishes would always arrive from Lupwe.

Following each party, Pete made sure to relate in his characteristic flair the details of each of these gatherings. Reading his letters, Tena must have almost felt as if she had been there. In describing the Christmas of 1938, Pete wrote.

> It all began when work was through on Saturday afternoon, and we combined our efforts and put up ye jolly old Christmas tree. Then began the speculation as to what St. Nick was going to bring, and whether we had been sufficiently good to deserve the gifts that we had asked for, or was there perhaps a chance to get only a big stick in our stockings. Well we proceeded very hopefully, and in the evening our firstborn and I did a little last minute buying, went to Grandma's and then to bed so that the jolly gentleman in red would not see our lights on and perhaps pass us up completely. The weather man played his part perfectly by giving a couple of light snow falls in as many days, and on Christmas Eve enough snow flew to just whiten things up for the sleigh and reindeer to smoothly pass along. We all of course hung up our stockings with care, in hopes that St. Nicholas soon would be there.

He did not disappoint us. The following morning we heard the girls stirring and Betty Jo softly calling, "Daddy, Daddy, it's Christmas Day." I jumped up and with that we all followed the little lady to the living room. It was all just too wonderful to see that Santa had brought her just the kind of piano and diddy doll that she wanted, and there was a lamp from Judy Nell for her chest of drawers, and a hat and glove outfit from Uncle Tom and Auntie Jennie. Then came her turn to surprise her Daddy and mother with the things that she had secretly bought and kept from the other. All this time while Betty Jo was busy unpacking, our littlest darling was pulling at the pretty paper and ribbons and just saying, "Pretty? Pretty?" When the excitement was all over and the senior sister had a bit of a breathing spell she said, "I bought you both something but what did you get for me?" Well, this was a very fair question because the things that we had given her had supposedly come from Santa Claus. We then told her that we were giving her the set of building blocks and also a junior chair that had not yet arrived. This satisfied her very well.

He went on for another several paragraphs, enumerating the gifts he gratefully received, recounting the sermon heard at church later that morning, and describing the Christmas dinner at Ma's house that was enjoyed by all.

Accompanying the fully-orbed descriptions of these grand holidays was also often a blessing. At Christmas 1952, Pete wrote to Tena,

I wish to extend to you our very best wishes for a most joyous Christmas season, and may the New Year also give you a very large measure of that inner joy, peace, and happiness that is so necessary to tranquil living. May the Good Lord, who has made Christmas a day of paramount importance in the life of the Christian, make that day and every succeeding day of the coming year so vital that we shall wish to make a daily spiritual trip to the stable of Bethlehem for adoration of the Saviour of Mankind.

In addition to the letters and gifts, there were also other ways to keep the family close. When Tena had left for Nigeria, the family had given her a movie camera, and the reels that she produced and sent home provided hours of enjoyment for her brothers and their families. Her video skills were at first underdeveloped, but with some advice from Pete, they improved over time! He wrote on December 22, 1937,

Brother Pete kept Tena in touch with the family at home by writing regularly.

Your films came yesterday and had a private showing before a very small but exclusive group. You have devoted much of your film to showing different groups standing around, and then telling them to walk to a certain point in order to get a little action on the picture. This can be just as well seen on your still photos. You do have some interesting bits interspersed throughout the film however, such as the boys playing leapfrog, and also where a whole group of men are carrying long poles as if they were about to build something. Now if you would have followed that right up and shown what they were building, how they built it, and then showed the finished product, you would have what Hollywood calls continuity in your plot. It is that kind of action that is so much preferred to the consciousness of being filmed.

By the following spring, he was congratulating Tena on the improvements she had made in her creativity, and in the technical aspects of exposure and camera angle.

Photographs were also an important means of contact. Many snapshots traveled back and forth between Lupwe and Chicago,

giving Tena a means to watch her nieces and nephews grow up. On
August 17, 1938, she wrote home,

> I have been looking at the snapshots which you sent,
> Pete. How bright little Sue looks and little Harry looks
> like he is going to whip all the boys in the neighborhood.
> He already looks like a prize fighter and certainly does
> not take after his father. We had a good laugh at the way
> Pete was holding Sue Anne. Betty Jo has grown in
> height since I left and she is beginning to look more and
> more like you Betty.

There was one last means that Tena was able to put to use for
staying in touch with the home folk. When the Smiths or Jennie
returned to America on furlough, Tena would often load them up
with letters, gifts, and best wishes to be delivered to loved ones in
person. When Jennie went home in 1938, Tena sent with her a
host of African memorabilia. Pete wrote on July 18, 1938,

> The other day brother Sam took a day off and went to
> Holland, Michigan. He nosed about for a cottage a bit,
> but I think that his main reason was to visit with Jennie
> Stielstra. When he returned early the same day he called
> us all on the phone and said that he was going to be at
> Ma's house with souvenirs and trophies from Africa. It
> was quite surprising that it worked out as slick as it did
> for everyone was on deck. Naturally there was a great
> deal of noise and finally it came to a division of the
> spoils. You had specified that Sam was to have the
> Python skin, so there was no choice there. But there
> were two bow and arrow sets with beautifully worked
> arrow containers that the three remaining boys eyed
> rather enviously. Well we drew lots to see who was to get
> an arrow set and who was to get the cheetah skin (I call
> it a cheetah, but I really don't know whether it is that or
> a young leopard, or possibly a wild cat. Will you please
> inform me as to the name and origin of the skin?). The
> die was cast and when the hands lifted from off the

coins, Harry and Tom were each the proud possessors of African hunting equipment, while on my living room floor lies the beautiful skin.

Sam really had no place to put a [Python] skin 14 feet long so he donated his trophy to Tom to hang in his office. Tom later gave Sam the bow and arrow set and so everybody is happy. And from your brother Pete a thousand thanks, dear Sister, for so nice a gift.

Jennie, like Tena's other colleagues when they came, was treated with a healthy dose of Huizenga hospitality when in the Chicago area and, in turn, provided the family with the latest news from Lupwe. When Jennie left to return to Nigeria later that year, they made sure that gifts accompanied her to reach Tena later. Pete wrote,

We put up a little box for you for Jennie to take back on her return home. To explain the situation I might say that each of us came with a neatly wrapped package, but when we started to put them together for compactness, each one lost its identity, which probably makes it a more communistic affair. The traveling bag that Jennie is taking, however, is from Tom. I have also sent for that [replacement] glass for your clock and had it sent COD right to Jennie ... because I had no way of determining its price.

Of course, not all of the news that traveled towards Nigeria and Tena's expectant ears was good news. She sometimes found herself lifting prayers heavenward for the growing children, and for the crises and problems her family at home periodically faced. While she could not be near, she knew that the God she served was, and it was into his hands that she entrusted their care.

The most difficult news, though, was the news that announced family illness and death. On September 21, 1945, Tena's brother Tom died of a heart attack while on holidays at age 44. A short telegram to Lupwe announced his passing, and Tena had to wait several weeks before the family letters arrived explaining the circumstances of his death and describing the funeral.

Less than two years later in the spring of 1947, Pete sent another telegram to Lupwe. When Tena read that her mother was failing fast, she immediately began making arrangements to move up the departure date for her forthcoming furlough. With what clearly appeared to be God's providence, details fell into place, and Tena was able to leave Lupwe on May 9. Only two days later, she lifted off from Nigeria in a Pan Am aircraft to arrive in Chicago on Wednesday, May 14. Rushing to the side of the woman who had been her step-mother for 32 years, Tena found herself holding Aaltje Huizenga's hand when she died at 2:30 P.M. the following day.

Death was to come to the Huizenga family one more time before Tena was to permanently leave Nigeria. On January 7, 1953, Pete began his letter to Tena:

> This morning I sent a cable off to you. This is the third time that I have been called on to do so. The Lord has felt, in his infinite wisdom, to have called to his eternal reward the soul that has dwelt in the person of Brother Sam.

It would be over a week before Tena received this letter, but the telegram arrived in three days on January 10. It read simply, "Brother Sam passed away today. Heart attack. Brother Pete."

Tena immediately responded,

> Your cablegram arrived a few hours ago. Mr. Holkeboer broke the news to me and it has left me stunned. Oh, if I could only be in your midst this afternoon as you entrust the body to its last resting place. In thought I am with you and it is at times like this that one feels the miles that separate us from one another.

> I am now eagerly awaiting your letter telling me the details. I know we were in a sense prepared that this

could happen and yet, when he seemed in good health of late, one just puts it from one's thoughts.

Our little group is very small now. Just the three of us left from that family group which still seemed so complete when our family picture was taken ...

Tuesday as I relived the scene of Pa's death 17 years ago I had no idea that what was once our parental home would again be cast into sorrow.

My heart is heavy tonight, but not far away the natives are having a dance and the tom toms and drums are going strong ...

It is nine o'clock Lupwe time and so about 3:00 P.M. Cicero time. As I see you gathered in church, oh how I long to cast one loving look on the body that lies so cold and lifeless before the pulpit. But such is not to be, so I will follow you in thought as you carry the mortal remains to its last resting place ...

Seeing you sign the cablegram "Brother Pete" struck a cord of love. You mean much to me Pete and the letters from all the various members of your family are cherished. At times I feel very lonely and I long for a home and family of my own. A single person does miss a great deal and I feel it more as I grow older. It is a good thing that we do not know what lies in store for us. God in His wisdom unveils each day at a time.

Just one year later, Tena would be making the decision to leave Lupwe and permanently rejoin the family she so missed and loved.

CHAPTER 12

New Beginnings

On February 16, 1954, Tena wrote:

Dear Members of the Mission Board:

Enclosed are the reports for the medical work at Lupwe and that of the leprosy work done at Gidan TerMeer.

As I write these reports there is a tinge of sadness associated with it. For, after having served for seventeen years on the Nigerian field, I feel the time has come when I must lay down my work and hand in my resignation. This past term has been a very busy one and often I did my work under physical handicaps, for throughout most of the term I have suffered from tropical ulcers on my leg. No sooner would one ulcer heal when another one would develop. This decision has been difficult to make and I have done so prayerfully.

It gives me real joy to be able to hand the work that has won my love to such capable people. Dr. Branderhorst hopes to start her work early in April and I'm sure that the work that was begun in a small way thirty years ago will grow into a gigantic task, especially when our hospital is built.

Looking back over my seventeen years of service in Nigeria, I thank God for what He has permitted me to do here. Many changes have taken place; Lupwe is no longer on the frontier line as it was in 1937. I also look back to the many pleasant associations which I have had with the Mission Board and with many of you as individuals. Be assured that as I resign from active duty, my interests shall always be with the work of our church in Nigeria.

There were hints for some time that Tena's resignation may be on the horizon. Even as early as January 1950, she was giving signs of being tired. In a letter to the Mission Board, she wrote at various points.

The medical work is very heavy at present ... To examine 64 new patients in one morning besides caring for many of them is a full schedule ... I do confess I often get the longing to get away for a few days but such opportunities do not present themselves .... T'is true that the responsibilities which are resting upon our shoulders are indeed heavy and sometimes it almost seems too heavy ... Our medical work among the lepers has grown so rapidly during the past year that it is hard to cope with it. We now have 575 lepers who we treat.

She felt stronger again after her fourth furlough but, in the fall of 1953, she was feeling tired again. Pete wrote on October 21,

I was not too much surprised when I read in one of your recent letters that this may be your last term on the field. I have felt that your enthusiasm for returning [from furlough] was not comparable to previous times. However, you have put in quite a stretch and I can well appreciate your willingness to leave it up to the newer members of the staff.

Over the years, the Lupwe staff continued to grow. Here
in 1949 or '50 are (*left to right*): Harry Boer, Anita
Vissia, Tena, Jennie Stielstra, Margaret Dykstra, and
Nelle and Ed Smith.

Two weeks later, Pete wrote again, this time touching on
something that had become a source of constant pain and
frustration,

> While I was in New Orleans last week your personal
> letter arrived in which you touch on different subjects ...
> I am disturbed that those miserable ulcers keep coming
> back to plague you.

In addition to these health concerns, it was indeed true that
things at Lupwe had changed. When the CRC had taken over the
mission field three years after Tena's arrival at the compound, the
average attendance at the Lupwe-Takum worship services was
about 200. One missionary would preach and lead the service
while others went out to preach at one of the dozen worship
centers that had been established in the surrounding villages. The
Johanna Veenstra Memorial Boarding School had 25 students on
its rolls, the day school, 34. Besides Ed and Nelle Smith, Jennie
Stielstra, and Tena, there were also 10 native evangelists.

In the fourteen years since, the work at Lupwe had exploded.
The field continued to expand as the CRC adopted part of the
Dutch Reformed Church's mission to the Tiv peoples. The native

church could now be characterized as indigenous, spiritual, self-supporting, disciplined, and itself a missionary church, reaching out to others with the gospel. There was a native church developing both amongst those who spoke the Hausa language and amongst the Tiv. The former consisted of eight congregations, each having its own elders, and one of them with its own ordained Pastor, Istifanus. Two additional congregations existed in the Tiv church. During the year 1953, 176 people made confession of faith to raise the number of communicant members in these congregations to 800. At least another 5,000 people, however, were gathered in the places of worship on any given Sunday morning. 43 Native evangelists and church workers helped to lead in worship and the work of the various congregations.

With six ordained men, seven educational teachers, two administrators, and eight medical workers, the mission had grown beyond Lupwe to now include several other mission stations as well.

Furthermore, a site for the mission's proposed hospital had already been selected in Takum. On a hill overlooking the city, the site was about five miles from the Lupwe compound. With this project on the horizon, more medical staff was being added to the mission team and, for the first time, Tena would be joined by doctors on the field.

In a sense, Tena felt like the work had outgrown her. In her years of service, she had helped bring the mission from infancy to maturity. It was time to leave.

Leaving, however, was not easy to do. On February 2, 1954, Tena wrote to Pete,

> People are beginning to ask me what I will do when I get home. I do not know as yet, but Henry Evenhouse has asked me whether I will do some deputation work for the [Missions] Board, to which I have consented. It is up my alley, as you know. That will give me a few months to think things through. As I near the end of my tour, it is exceedingly hard for me to bid farewell to friends and natives. The natives do not know as yet of my decision and only a very few of my friends know about it. I'm

hesitant about mentioning it. It has a tone of sadness to it and I am so apt to go into tears of late. I have gone through a hard tour and at times I was afraid that my nerves wouldn't hold out ... but praise the Lord I am well and my ulcer is better although it has left a nasty scar.

Two weeks later, on February 15, she wrote to Pete,

This coming week I hope to send in my letter of resignation. It is hard to do so, but I feel that I have to. Another ulcer is making her appearance and I've been having them right along ... As to the future, that is in the Lord's hands.

The "future" was to arrive only two short months later when she found herself once again in Chicago. Home for good, she wrote to the members of the Mission office staff on April 26, 1954:

Greetings from Berwyn! Yes, I arrived here yesterday and what a reception I did get! A huge cake which had "Welcome Sister to Our Home" as well as flowers adorned the table. The whole family of about twenty met me at the train at nine in the morning. I was astonished to see them, for I thought they would all be in church, but they played hooky for once.

Tena lived with Pete and Betty while she did some deputation work and tried to decide where the Lord was leading her next. She had maintained some interest in anesthetics ever since she had taken the course in anesthesiology after graduating from Moody, waiting to go overseas. Late in 1954, she decided to get some more anesthesia training and soon learned that the medical field had greatly expanded its repertoire of surgical techniques since her early nursing training. She wrote to the Mission Board staff in December 1954,

[The training is] sometimes nerve wracking. I have in mind when the patient decides to stop breathing a while,

which happens sometimes. The operations which are
performed are amazing! They actually do a general
overhauling in some cases and they even put in peep
holes in the head. Yesterday I saw an [operation] and as
I saw the surgeon at work, it looked more like a
carpenter for he was drilling holes in the head and then
took a peek at the brain!

Lupwe, this wasn't! Nevertheless, Tena completed her course
and by January 1955, she had accepted a position at the Health
Center in Allegan, Michigan, as an anesthetist.

She found a cozy home on Thomas Street and then asked
brother Pete if he would compose some poetry that could serve as
an invitation to friends and family alike to come visit her. Pete
responded with a poem that fit the bill perfectly:

Since my work in Africa is done
And I've had some time for rest and fun
I felt that I should find a spot
Where I could help the sick a lot.

Just such a place showed up for me
In a very neat Michigan community
The town of Allegan, so clean and neat
Is where I found my work and my retreat.

The people there had on their list
The need of an anesthetist
I filled this bill to their content
So moved right in and pitched my tent.

The place will most easily be found;
By mailman, guests or lazy hound
If you just ask a native, just any one you meet
Just where is One Six Nine on Thomas Street.

So come in and share with me
A bit of native hospitality

If this you cannot do at all
Then send a note or place a call.

The door will always be ajar
To friends both near and from afar
But try to come and have a see
And join me in some good conviviality

Tena's experience in Allegan, however, was at best bittersweet. Already in February, Tena was sensing a cause for concern regarding her standing at the Health Center. And then, on March 31, she wrote Pete and Betty:

The blow has come and that rather unexpectedly. Yesterday I was called into the Office and told that the doctors thought it advisable that I sever my connection with the hospital. Things had been going quite nicely and I thought that I might be able to stay until I heard definitely from the Board of Anesthetists. I think one of the reasons that it came at this time was because last week I had a child who suddenly stopped breathing on me in the beginning of an anesthetic and we had to give him oxygen. That upset the Doctor quite a bit, but it was no fault of mine. He had been standing right there when I gave the anesthetic and no sooner had he turned his back and the child just stopped breathing. He came to in a few minutes but it was upsetting to all of us concerned, but I felt that it was something outside of my control. It is just such things like that that make me wonder whether I want to stay in the field of anesthesiology. Last night as I was thinking things through I asked myself the question whether I wanted to spend the rest of my life in the operating room, working with people with whom one doesn't have a vital contact with. For one sees the patient just a few minutes before the operation and then the next personal contact is when they are recovering. I haven't come to a conclusion as yet, but through it all I have a peace which I myself cannot understand ... A month ago when I first heard about this possibility I was quite upset emotionally, but now I am quite reconciled to it ...

What the future holds for me I do not know. It all seems so very uncertain, but I'm calm about it and not emotionally upset. I'm praying much about these things and perhaps I must leave Allegan, although I have enjoyed my little house. It has been very lonely here, much more so than in Africa, for there we had at least eight workers close to one another, but here I have been alone quite a bit ... I am happy that I can face the future, knowing that all these things do not happen by chance, and yet, one cannot help but ask the question, "Why, Lord?"

Two weeks later, she again wrote to Pete and Betty:

Thinking it through I'm glad that I am leaving Allegan, much as I do enjoy my little house. Life would have been pretty lonely for me here and living alone like this is far from desirable. I just wasn't made to enjoy life by myself.

For a couple weeks, it looked like she might be returning to her old alma mater, Moody Bible Institute, to work in the infirmary. But then, the Medical Bureau contacted her with regards to an opportunity in Evergreen Park. She accepted their offer. When she began work as a Nurse Anesthetist at Little Company of Mary Hospital, and moved into her apartment at 1901 South Euclid Avenue, her new life in America had begun.

CHAPTER 13

Life on the South Side

Some effort was necessary if Tena was to successfully readjust to the American way of life. A basic old bicycle would not serve on the south side of Chicago as it had in Lupwe, and Tena soon found that a driver's license and car were essentials of life in the big city. After obtaining her license, Tena was soon on the road, but the driving school she attended had made little progress in improving her motoring skills or her poor eyesight. As a result, driving with Tena was always an adventure. Friends and family would stand on the curb to wave goodbye to Tena after a visit, inwardly cringing as they watched her precariously weave her way down the street. Her great-nephew, Wayne Jr., recalls one of his trips in the back seat of Aunt Tena's old Plymouth Duster. They were traveling down one of Chicago's expressways when a police car made its appearance and began flashing its lights at Tena. After pulling over, she watched in the mirror as the officer approached her car. Peering through her window, he explained, "The minimum speed limit along this stretch is 45 mph and you're barely doing 35! People are blowing their horns at you and barreling on past; you're a real hazard out here!"

When the occasion called for it, however, Tena was able to find the accelerator and use it. She wrote to her brother Harry near the end of 1956,

> I was standing still waiting for a truck to pass me, and in doing so, he hit me and put a dint in the back of my car.

I [went] after him, but after traveling five miles ... I gave
up the chase. And, of course, I can't collect insurance on
it!

There were other adjustments facing Tena upon her return to
Chicago as well. She needed to recognize that conducting business
in approximations was not as acceptable in America as it had been
in Nigeria. Pete had handled all of Tena's finances while she was
on the mission field and he promised to continue to assist her once
she was home. However, shortly after she sent him her tax
information for the year 1954, she received a reply from Pete dated
March 14, 1955:

Dear Sister:
When we deal with Uncle Sam, we don't get the benefit
of being permitted to guess at things. He wants
everything to figure out the way they happen. For
example, he is not satisfied to know you got "about"
$2,400.00 from the Mission Board! He wants the exact
figure plus the withholding slip that each employer must
furnish to an employee.

Pete went on to explain,

If you get anything that has to do with tax payments or
possible deductions, do not throw them away! Get into a
habit of putting all data in a file so that at the end of the
year you can sit down and systematically prepare a
comprehensible list of needed information.

Driving and taxes were parts of American life that Tena was
inevitably forced to adopt as her own. She resisted, however, ever
succumbing to the demands of American styles in dress and
fashion. She never owned jewelry, and her wardrobe reflected a
desire for affordability, comfort, and adaptability. Tena was a
woman of substance, but certainly never of style.

As she settled into her work at Little Company of Mary
Hospital, she decided to pursue some further studies on the side.

She worked six nights a week, with Sundays off. Three nights, she was on call from 7:00 to 7:00, and the other three nights from 11:00 to 7:00. The studies she pursued in the daytime, however, soon qualified her for other positions and, in the spring of 1957, she began working for the Holland Home for the elderly. She wrote to Harry on May 4, 1957,

> Greetings from your sister, who now talks just a little louder than usual, and who will step close to everyone and almost speaks in the other person's ear. I have had three days with the old folks and so far, I sort of like it. I am the administrator and am in charge of all the personnel, from the engineer to the nurses. I'll be having Saturdays and Sundays off.

Her new position demanded that she continue to update her education and in February 1959, she received a diploma certificate from MacNeal Memorial Hospital in Berwyn indicating that she had completed a six week refresher course for registered nurses.

Tena (*top right*) graduated from nursing refresher course at MacNeal Memorial Hospital.

Her work and schooling, however, were not all that kept her busy in her new life. She became a volunteer again at the Helping Hand Mission in downtown Chicago, the very same place where she had felt her call shaped earlier in life. At least once a month, she found herself before the men who had gathered at the Shelter that evening, exercising her unique talent for preaching. Periodically, she also continued to contribute articles to the *Banner* or the *Instructor*, and to travel to churches to speak of the continued need for missions in Africa and around the world.

Her interest in missions had remained keen, and she maintained two file boxes that she cross-referenced. One box listed all the missionaries that the CRC supported around the globe, while the other box contained a record of each of the denomination's active mission fields. Despite her broad interest in missions, however, the Nigerian field naturally remained her first love. In addition to supporting various mission projects in Nigeria, like the new hospital in Takum, she also continued to sponsor the education of some of the friends and colleagues she had known when there. One of these individuals was Ali Nyita, whom she continued to send money for until he graduated in November of 1959. To help celebrate the occasion, Tena sent him a special gift. Ali had been one of Tena's houseboys in the late 1940's and she was thrilled with his ambition to become a pastor in the Nigerian church. After he graduated, he returned to Baissa to teach until a new class was able to open at the Theological College of Northern Nigeria.

Tena also made sure to take some time for herself. In 1961, she fulfilled another of her dreams: to visit the Holy Land. Her post cards home tell of her experiences there, including a morning service in the Garden Tomb and a vesper service on Mount Olivet.

Yet, despite the demands of work and study, of church and volunteer service, of mission interest and travel, family still played a leading role in Tena's life after her return from Nigeria. Only two and a half years after Tena had begun to enjoy being reunited with the family, her lifetime confidant and brother, Pete, died on September 1, 1956 of an angina attack. He was 47 years old. Pete's passing left only Tena and Harry from the original Huizenga clan, along with three sisters-in-law.

The diminished size of the family, however, did little to diminish the frequency of the Sunday get togethers after church or other times of celebration. As the self-appointed family historian, Tena would bring jars of pennies to each of the family's gatherings in order to play the "family history game" with her great nieces and nephews. While dinner was being prepared, these younger ones would encircle Tena trying to answer her questions. "How many brothers did your grandfather on your mother's side have?" "What were their names?" "In what year was your Uncle born?" "Who is your mother's youngest sibling?" For each question the children answered correctly, they were given one of Aunt Tena's pennies. When the questions related to kin were exhausted, Tena would ask Bible trivia questions, similarly rewarding answers that were right. Finally, the pennies would be put away and Tena would intrigue the children with stories about the family until dinner was ready. She assured these youngsters that somewhere, somehow, there had to be royalty in the Huizenga line.

Tena enjoyed traveling in her years following Lupwe.

Due to circumstances, Tena had the opportunity to influence two of her great-nephews more directly. In the late 1960's, while their mother underwent repeated surgeries, Wayne Jr. and Scott spent many weekends at their Aunt's apartment on Euclid Avenue. Always taking advantage of every opportunity to instill a sense of family ties in the younger generation, Tena would make the boys write a letter to someone in the family on her old typewriter each

L-r: Betty Bovenkerk Huizenga, Ella Huizenga Taylor
(daughter of Siert and Sam Huizenga), Bertha
Wezeman, and Tena

time they were in her care. She made sure their word usage was
correct and would send them to the dictionary when their spelling
seemed erroneous.

These literary skills were not the only ones Tena wanted to
convey to Wayne Jr. and Scott. She taught them how to knit,
crochet, and even cook on her old gas stove. Sunny-Side-Up eggs
became the boy's specialty, which they made in a little ring that sat
in Tena's frying pan. Tena's refrain each time a new egg was
cracked was, "Don't let any of the shells get in!" There were other
cooking experiments, too. Making fudge was another favorite,
especially given the fact that the recipe's specifications for sugar
were invariably exceeded!

In December each year, Tena took the boys downtown on the
"L" train to Marshall Fields to do some Christmas shopping and to
look at the window fronts which had been dressed up to celebrate
the season. After buying some caramel corn from a street vendor,
they would stand in line at the bank to see Santa Claus and to get
their pictures taken sitting on the jolly old gent's lap.

Even beyond the family gatherings, and her special care of
Wayne Jr. and Scott, Tena made great efforts to keep the family
close. She was constantly making scarves, quilts, slippers, and

other accessories for those she loved, and these gifts would provide her with the perfect opportunity for a visit. Tena would appear at the door, bearing not only her handiwork, but often a treat, an article she had clipped, or a book to lend as well. If she had been invited to stay, she would also have her own sheets with her so as to impose as little a burden on her hosts as possible. And, as always, she would have the latest family news to share.

In turn, Tena's apartment door was also always open. While the apartment may have been somewhat unkempt and exuded a unique "odor of time," it was nevertheless a place where one could always experience warm hospitality and hear countless tales of adventure and misadventure. The stories were typically connected somehow with the odd objects and miscellaneous items that adorned her apartment shelves and bookcases.

The apartment remained home for Tena for 23 years until 1978, when she died in her own bedroom.

CHAPTER 14

A Life that Lives On

In Nigeria, Tena had stood by the side of many as they breathed their last breath. In the fall of 1977, however, Tena was forced to consider her own mortality. She had developed lung cancer, and the abominable disease had begun to take its toll. On October 13, 1977, she wrote to Jennie, who had returned home two years after Tena, and other "dear ones" in Holland, Michigan, to update them on her ongoing treatment.

> Yesterday I went to my lung specialist, who returned from his vacation in Russia. In consultation with my doctor they had decided to bronchoscope my left lung. This means that I will have to go to our local hospital on Monday, Oct. 17 and if all goes well, I will be able to return within 24 hours. My cough is still with me and something has to be done to check it. The x-rays showed many shadows, which they didn't understand. I dread the procedure. They will anesthetize the trachea locally, so that I may help them with swallowing a tube, the size of a pencil. Then they will look into the lung with a light. I have never seen it done, but the procedure will be done in surgery.
>
> As you gather for prayer next Monday evening, I covet your prayers.

A month later, she wrote these friends again.

> I've finished my sixteenth treatment and I'm beginning
> to feel the effects of them. The x-ray, which was taken a
> week ago, was disappointing because it showed the fluid
> which had accumulated in the left lung and therefore
> didn't show what radiation was doing to the tumor. As
> long as my breathing is not too troublesome they will
> leave the fluid there until the radiation is finished and
> then my lung specialist will have to tap it again. In
> September, he drew 850 cc from the lung.
>
> My appetite is still poor but thus far [I have not
> experienced any nausea]. Presently I'm troubled with
> muscle spasms and they are painful and cause me to be
> awake many an hour during the night.

The last line of the letter, however, best described the extent
of her suffering because Tena, the emissary of family sociability,
was forced to reject an invitation for one of the Huizenga holiday
dinners.

> I've been invited to have Thanksgiving Day dinner with
> Betty's family, but just now I prefer to be left alone,
> seeing food has no appeal to me.

On Thanksgiving Day, she wrote her friends in Holland
again,

> I spent the day at home by choice. I wasn't up to being
> with many people. So my neighbor brought me over a
> plate of turkey and other foods, which I couldn't do
> justice to because of my failing appetite.
>
> Yesterday I had to drink more than a glass of barium in
> connection with an esophagus x-ray. What a terrible
> experience that was! If all goes well, Monday will be the
> last day of treatment. I'll not know until the doctor tells

me so on Monday. Then on Wednesday I'm scheduled for a bone marrow scan. And if all goes well, I'll be transferred to my lung specialist for further treatment. I think I still have fluid in the left cavity, so that will have to be drawn out.

Yesterday and today I've been pushing fluids to get rid of the barium which I had to drink. What a chore that is.

I have many reasons to be thankful on this day, but oh at times the nights are so long for my arthritis has been causing me quite a bit of pain.

She concluded the letter with a simple statement of confidence,

I'm trusting the Lord for each day and the prayers of loved ones have sustained me.

As Tena's condition deteriorated, the friends and family that she had given so much of her life to rallied around her to insure that she was able to stay in her small apartment. Her nephew Peter hired some nurses to furnish in-home medical care, while her niece, Betty Jo, came each day to schedule and supervise the nursing care, and to offer Tena a familial presence.

Many of the nurses, like Jeanette VanderWelde, were Tena's old friends from nursing school or Moody. One would be scheduled to work early each morning and would be replaced later by a nurse who would work late into the evening. Betty Jo would drive the half hour route each morning from LaGrange to Tena's apartment, arriving by 10:00. She would typically stay until dinner, but, the weather was so bad that winter that she often stayed overnight. One night, after a particularly heavy snowfall, Betty Jo was sure the scheduled nurse would not be able to make it that day. Nevertheless, the Moody nurse was at the apartment door on time, having trekked several blocks through the knee deep snow in order to be there.

Many others pitched in too. Her nieces Ella and Janet came frequently to sit, and when Tena began rejecting food and water, her nephew-in-law Frank would bring medicated popsicles.

Tena was unable to speak the last month of her life, but she enjoyed listening to the musical tapes that friends and family brought. She did manage to squeeze out a few words in her final days, however. At one point, as Betty Jo was singing camp songs to her, Tena opened one eye and simply said, "No." A few days later, she was calling out, "Mamma!"

Betty Jo knew the end must be near and she put the word out to the family that Tena probably only had three to four earthly days left. Brother Harry, who was in Hong Kong at the time, immediately left for Chicago and joined the family at the apartment. Although Tena could not respond verbally, it was clear she knew that Harry had joined them and, the next day, Saturday, January 28, 1978, she died holding Betty Jo's hand. The following month, she would have been 71 years old.

Twenty-third Psalm	In Loving Memory of
The Lord is my shepherd; I shall not want.	Tena Huizenga
He maketh me to lie down in green pastures: he leadeth me beside the still waters.	†
He restoreth my soul; he leadeth me in the paths of righteousness for his name's sake.	Born FEBRUARY 26, 1907
Yea, though I walk through the valley of the shadow of death, I will fear no evil: for thou art with me; thy rod and thy staff they comfort me.	Passed Away SAT., JANUARY 28th, 1978 Services Held at MULDER MEMORIAL CHAPELS
Thou preparest a table before me in the presence of mine enemies; thou anointest my head with oil; my cup runneth over.	TUESDAY, JAN. 31st, 1978 ONE P.M. Officiating REV. HENRY EVENHOUSE
Surely goodness and mercy shall follow me all the days of my life: and I will dwell in the house of the Lord for ever.	Interment FOREST HOME CEMETERY

The "In Memoriam" card printed for Tena's funeral.

It was a peaceful death: Tena died as she had lived, with a quiet and sure confidence that her life was in the Lord's hands.

Over 350 friends and family visited the Mulder Funeral Home in Cicero where Tena lay and, three days later, her lifetime friend and colleague, Rev. Henry Evenhouse, led the funeral service celebrating Tena's life. He preached from the book of Matthew, chapter 9, verse 38: "Ask the Lord of the harvest, therefore, to send out workers into His harvest field." He spoke of the call that God had placed on Tena's life and of how she had lived out that call as a person sent by God. She had recognized her calling as something that permeated all of her life, not just her years in Nigeria. The sermon was concluded by recalling how Tena had left an eternal legacy of faith and commitment.

Tena took many things with her to her grave at Forest Home Cemetery in Forest Park, Illinois. Her animated and vivacious presence would no longer be enjoyed by the family on Sunday afternoons and holidays, the cheer that her cards and notes and gifts brought to many would be missed, and her ministry to the lonely and outcast would be gone.

She would also, however, leave many things behind. Her entire estate, worth a quarter million dollars, was left to Christian charitable causes. The Nigerian Ekas Benue church, which Tena had invested her life in, had blossomed into the indigenous and self-governing church that Tena had always prayed it would become. The Nigerian people she had served were now serving others as nurses, teachers, and pastors. The sense of family she had always hoped to instill was enshrined in a short history that she had written and the family's heritage and tradition were celebrated at a huge family reunion in Holland in 1993. Her traits of generosity and caring for the lonely were also adopted and carried on by the Huizenga family.

Lastly, the memories of Tena live on in the lives of her family from which they draw strength and encouragement to face the new day.

APPENDIX

Timeline of Tena's life

1865 May 6, Altje Kremer born in Uithuizen, Groningen.
1868 May 11, Harm Huizenga born in 't Zandt, Groningen.
1893 Harm Huizenga emigrates to America.
1897 Harm returns to the Netherlands to marry Altje Kremer. They return to America and settle in Chicago's West Side.
1898 January 29, brother Siert (Sam) is born.
1901 December 22, brother Tammes (Tom) is born.
1907 February 26, Tena is born.
1908 October 31, brother Petro (Peter) is born.
1913 March 22, Altje (Tena's mother) dies.
1914 Harm and his four children move back to the Netherlands.
1915 February 14, Harm marries Aaltje Keizer.
1916 June 28, brother Gerrit Harry is born.
1916 October, Harm, Aaltje, and five children move to Chicago.
1917-1925 Tena attends Ebenezer Christian School, Austin High School (evening classes).
1925 Tena begins three-year program at the Chicago Mission Training School, then Garfield Park Hospital.
1933 May 24, Tena graduates from Garfield Park Community Hospital Training School for Nurses.
1933 Tena at Moody Bible Institute, graduates in 1935.
1935 February, in Chicago, Tena has heart-to-heart talk with Jennie Stielstra, about missionary work in Nigeria.
1936 January 6, Harm dies in Cicero, Illinois.
1937 February 27, Tena sails from New York.
1937 March 31, Tena arrives in Lupwe.

1937 May 27 to June 18, Tena conducts her first trek into various towns and villages.

1937 December 12, Tena preaches for the first time.

1938 August 6, first electricity in Lupwe.

1939 January 6, Tena passed her grueling Hausa exam, pending completion of her first sermon in the Hausa language, which was finished on February 10.

1939 March 14, Peter H. Huizenga is born.

1939 June 10, Tena leaves Nigeria for furlough, arrives New York August 1.

1940 March, Tena sails from New York, returning to Nigeria, arrives Lagos on May 27.

1941 Tena is the only registered nurse at the mission station.

1943 April 6, Tena leaves Nigeria for furlough.

1943 June 10, Tena arrives in New York.

1944 August 19, Tena returns to Nigeria.

1945 September 21, brother Tom dies.

1947 May 9, Tena departs Lupwe, arrives Chicago May 14.

1947 May 15, Aaltje dies.

1947 November, Tena returns to Nigeria.

1950 December 18, Tena arrives in the United States for her final furlough, after visiting Italy, Switzerland, and Holland on the way home.

1951 July 27, Tena leaves for her final term in Nigeria.

1951 October 29, lightning strikes dispensary and burns it down.

1953 January 7, brother Sam dies.

1954 February (?), Tena resigns from missionary service in Africa.

1954 Fall, Tena takes course in anesthesiology.

1955 January, Tena begins work as an anesthetist at Health Center, Allegan, Michigan.

1955 March, Tena resigns from job in Allegan.

1955 Tena begins work as nurse anesthetist at Little Company of Mary Hospital; she lived on South Euclid Avenue, Chicago.

1956 September 1, brother Peter dies.

1957 Spring,Tena begins work at Holland Home for the elderly.

1958 November, the frontier dispensary in Lupwe is closed.

1959 Tena completes refresher course for registered nurses at MacNeal Memorial Hospital in Berwyn.

1961 Tena visits the Holy Land.
1977 Tena diagnosed with lung cancer.
1978 January 28, Tena dies in Chicago.

Van Raalte Institute Mission Statement and Publications

Mission Statement

The Van Raalte Institute is a department of Hope College. Hence, its mission relates directly to and supports the mission of Hope College, an undergraduate liberal arts institution offering academic programs in the context of the historic Christian faith.

The Van Raalte Institute of Hope College honors the memory and vision of Reverend Dr. Albertus C. Van Raalte, the founder of Holland, Michigan, by engaging in and promoting the study of his life and legacy, exploring the cultural history of the West Michigan community, and publishing, through the Van Raalte Press, scholarly work on Dutch immigration and heritage in North America and around the globe.

The institute derives its vision from a letter dated November 27, 1846, by A. C. Van Raalte, written shortly after his party landed in New York. As he was headed westward, he declared "I hope that a large colony can be established here in America which will focus its work on the Kingdom of God." His vision also extended far beyond the boundaries of Holland, Michigan, to other colonies and to immigrants throughout the United States. The bold Christian vision that he had for the church, for education, and for the community continues to have an impact on the "colony" that he founded on February 9, 1847, and on the college which he helped to establish fifteen years later.

The institute carries out its educational mission not only through research and publication but also through the sponsorship of lectures and presentations by its members and invited guests. Through liaison with scholars and educational and cultural institutions in the Netherlands and other countries, the institute seeks to promote the understanding of the history of this community. From time to time, the institute will host visiting scholars from these countries to enable them to engage in research in our local archives and to provide a broader perspective to our own endeavors.

Publications of the Van Raalte Institute

The following are publications by senior and visiting research fellows and other associates of the Van Raalte Institute, 1994-2023

Aay, Henk. *American Eyes on the Netherlands: Film, Public Diplomacy, and Dutch Identity, 1943-74, including a Survey of Dutch Visual Media in America from the 17th to the 21st Century*. Van Raalte Press, forthcoming.

———, Janny Venema, Dennis Voskuil, eds. *Sharing Pasts: Dutch Americans through Four Centuries*. Van Raalte Press, 2017.

Baer, Marc, and Allison Utting. *Making Music: Hope College's Music Department, A History*. Van Raalte Press, 2020.

Bruins, Elton J., Karen G. Schakel, Sara Fredrickson Simmons, and Marie N. Zingle. *Albertus and Christina: The Van Raalte Family, Home and Roots*. Eerdmans, 2004.

———. *The Americanization of a Congregation*. 2nd ed. Eerdmans, 1995.

———, and Karen G. Schakel, eds. *Envisioning Hope College: Letters Written by Albertus C. Van Raalte to Philip Phelps Jr., 1857 to 1875*. Van Raalte Press; Eerdmans, 2011.

Bruggink, Donald J., Dennis N. Voskuil, and William Katerberg, eds. *Dutch Immigrant Stories*. Van Raalte Press, 2022.

Cox, John D. *The City in Its Heart: The First 100 Years of Maple Avenue Ministries, Holland, Michigan, 1913-2013*. Van Raalte Press, 2014.

Dickason, David G. *Faith, Hope, and Love: The Hakeem's Journey*. Van Raalte Press, 2022.

Ester, Peter, Nella Kennedy, and Earl Wm. Kennedy, eds. *The American Diary of Jacob Van Hinte, Author of the Classic Immigrant Study* Nederlanders in Amerika. Van Raalte Press; Eerdmans, 2010.

———. *Faith, Family, and Fortune: Reformed Upbringing and Calvinist Values of Highly Successful Dutch American Entrepreneurs*. Van Raalte Press, 2012.

Fessler, Paul, Hubert R. Krygsman, and Robert P. Swierenga, eds. *Dutch Immigrants on the Plains*. The Association for the Advancement of Dutch American Studies, 2005.

Harinck, George, and Hans Krabbendam. *Sharing the Reformed Tradition: The Dutch-North American Exchange, 1846-1996*. VU Uitgeverij, 1996.

———. *'We Live Presently under a Waning Moon,' Nicolaus Martin Steffens as Leader of the Reformed Church in America in the West in Years of Transition (1878-1895)*. Van Raalte Press, 2013.

Heideman, Eugene P. *The Canons of Dort: God's Freedom, Justice, and Persistence*. Ed. Donald J. Bruggink. Van Raalte Press, 2023.

———. *Hendrik P. Scholte: His Legacy in the Netherlands and in America*. Van Raalte Press; Eerdmans, 2015.

———. *The Practice of Piety: The Theology of the Midwestern Reformed Church in America, 1866-1966*. Eerdmans, 2009.

Hemenway, Stephen. *Hope Beyond Borders: The Life and Letters of Paul Fried*. Van Raalte Press, 2014.

Heusinkveld, Paul. *Elephant Baseball: A Missionary Kid's Tale*. Eerdmans, 2017.

———, with Margaret Doorenbos. *Margaret's Mission to Arabia, Africa, and India 1965-2010*. Van Raalte Press, 2021.

Jacobson, Jeanne M., Elton J. Bruins, and Larry J. Wagenaar. *Albertus C. Van Raalte: Dutch Leader and American Patriot*. Hope College, 1996.

Japinga, Lynn. *Loyalty and Loss: The Reformed Church in America, 1945-1994*. Eerdmans, 2013.

Kennedy, Earl Wm. *A Commentary on the Minutes of the Classis of Holland, 1848-76: A Detailed Record of Persons and Issues, Civil and Religious, in the Dutch Colony of Holland, Michigan*. 3 vols. Van Raalte Press, 2018.

——, Donald A. Luidens, and David Zwart, eds. *Dutch Muck—and Much More: Dutch Americans in Farming, Religion Art, and Astronomy*. Van Raalte Press, 2019.

Kennedy, James C., and Caroline J. Simon. *Can Hope Endure: An Historical Case Study in Christian Higher Education*. Eerdmans, 2005.

Kennedy, Nella, Mary Risseeuw, and Robert P. Swierenga, eds. *Diverse Destinies: Dutch* Kolonies *in Wisconsin and the East*. Van Raalte Press, 2012.

Krabbendam, Hans. *Freedom on the Horizon: Dutch Immigration to America, 1840-1940*. Eerdmans, 2009.

Kraft, George. *A Place to Call Home: A Missionary Kid's Tale*. Van Raalte Press, 2022.

Luidens, Donald A., Donald J. Bruggink, and Herman J. De Vries Jr., eds. *Dutch Reformed Education: Immigrant Legacies in North America*. Van Raalte Press, 2020.

——, and JoHannah M. Smith, eds. *Jack: A Compassionate Compendium. A Tribute to Dr. Jacob E. Nyenhuis: Scholar, Servant, Leader*. Van Raalte Press, 2018.

——. *Seeds of Hope, Hate, and Change: Missionary Witnesses to the Middle East in Transition*. 2 vols. Van Raalte Press, 2020.

Nyenhuis, Jacob E. *et alii*. *Hope College at 150: Anchored in Faith, Educating for Leadership and Service in a Global Society*. Van Raalte Press, 2019.

——, Suzanne M. Sinke, and Robert P. Swierenga, eds. *Across Borders: Dutch Migration to North America and Australia*. Van Raalte Press, 2010.

——, Robert P. Swierenga, and Lauren M. Berka, eds. *Aunt Tena: Called to Serve, Journals and Letters of Tena A. Huizenga, Missionary Nurse to Nigeria*. Eerdmans, 2009.

——. *Centennial History of the Fourteenth Street Christian Reformed Church, Holland, Michigan, 1902-2002*. Holland, Michigan, 2002.

——. *Fourteenth Street Christian Reformed Church: 110th Anniversary Booklet*. Van Raalte Press, 2012.

———, and Jeanne M. Jacobson. *A Dream Fulfilled: The Van Raalte Sculpture in Centennial Park*. Hope College, 1997.

———, and George Harinck. *The Enduring Legacy of Albertus C. Van Raalte as Leader and Liaison*. Van Raalte Press; Eerdmans, 2014.

———, eds. *A Goodly Heritage: Essays in Honor of the Reverend Dr. Elton J. Bruins at Eighty*. Eerdmans, 2007.

———. *Myth and the Creative Process: Michael Ayrton and the Myth of Daedalus, the Maze Maker*. Wayne State University Press, 2003.

Parr, Judy. *Hope Church: Holland, Michigan. The First 150 Years, 1862 -2012*. Van Raalte Press, 2012.

Renner, Thomas L. *In Pursuit of Excellence. Be Strong—Be True: A History of Intercollegiate Athletics at Hope College, 1970–2020*. 2 vols. Van Raalte Press, 2022.

Sheeres, Janet Sjaarda. *The Not-So-Promised Land: The Dutch in Amelia County, Virginia, 1868-1880*. Eerdmans, 2013.

———. *Son of Secession: Douwe J. Vander Werp*. Eerdmans, 2006.

Stellingwerff, Johan. *Iowa Letters: Dutch Immigrants on the American Frontier*. Ed. Robert P. Swierenga. Trans. Walter Lagerwey. Eerdmans, 2003.

Swierenga, Robert P. *A. C. Van Raalte: Pastor by Vocation, Entrepreneur by Necessity*. Van Raalte Press, 2023.

———, Nella Kennedy, and Lisa Zylstra, eds. *Dutch Americans and War: United States and Abroad*. Van Raalte Press, 2014.

———, Jacob E. Nyenhuis, and Nella Kennedy, eds. *Dutch American Arts and Letters in Historical Perspective*. Van Raalte Press, 2008.

———. *Dutch Chicago: A History of the Hollanders in the Windy City*. Eerdmans, 2002.

———, Donald Sinnema, and Hans Krabbendam, eds., *The Dutch in Urban America*. The Association for the Advancement of Dutch American Studies, 2004.

———. *Elim: A Chicago Christian School and Life Training Center for the Disabled*. Eerdmans, 2005.

——. *Faith and Family: Dutch Immigration and Settlement in the United States, 1820-1920.* Homes & Meier, 2000.

——. *His Faithfulness Continues: A History of Timothy Christian Schools of Chicagoland.* Van Raalte Press, 2020.

——. and Elton J. Bruins. *Family Quarrels in the Dutch Reformed Churches in the Nineteenth Century.* Eerdmans, 1999.

——. and Joel Lefever, eds. *For Food and Faith, Dutch Immigration to Western Michigan, 1846-1960.* Van Raalte Institute; Holland Museum, 2000.

——, and Jacob E. Nyenhuis, eds. *Historic Dutch Sites in the Holland/Zeeland Area: An Illustrated Tour Guide.* Van Raalte Press, 2015.

——. *Holland, Michigan: From Dutch Colony to Dynamic City.* 3 vols. Van Raalte Press; Eerdmans, 2014.

——, Adriaan de Wit, and Gordon De Young, eds. *Netherlanders in America: A Study of Emigration and Settlement in the Nineteenth and Twentieth Centuries in the United States of America,* by Jacob Van Hinte. The Historical Committee of the Christian Reformed Church, 2003.

——. and William Van Appledorn, eds. *Old Wing Mission: Cultural Interchange as Chronicled by George and Arvilla Smith in their Work with Chief Wakazoo's Ottawa Band on the West Michigan Frontier.* Eerdmans, 2008.

Van den Broeke, Leon. *"Pope of the Classis"? The Leadership of Albertus C. Van Raalte in Dutch and American Classes.* Van Raalte Press, 2011.

Verhave, Jan Peter. *A Constant State of Emergency: Paul de Kruif, Microbe Hunter and Health Activist.* Van Raalte Press, 2020.

INDEX

Made in the USA
Middletown, DE
29 October 2023

41489107R00080